crime, punishment and migration

Dario Melossi

Los Angeles | London | New Delhi
Singapore | Washington DC

Los Angeles | London | New Delhi
Singapore | Washington DC

SAGE Publications Ltd
1 Oliver's Yard
55 City Road
London EC1Y 1SP

SAGE Publications Inc.
2455 Teller Road
Thousand Oaks, California 91320

SAGE Publications India Pvt Ltd
B 1/I 1 Mohan Cooperative Industrial Area
Mathura Road
New Delhi 110 044

SAGE Publications Asia-Pacific Pte Ltd
3 Church Street
#10-04 Samsung Hub
Singapore 049483

© Dario Melossi 2015

First published 2015

Editor: Natalie Aguilera/Amy Jarrold
Assistant editor: James Piper/George Knowles
Production editor: Sarah Cooke
Copyeditor: Elaine Leek
Proofreader: Lynda Watson
Indexer: Silvia Benvenuto
Marketing manager: Sally Ransom
Cover design: Francis Kenney
Typeset by: C&M Digitals (P) Ltd, Chennai, India
Printed and bound by CPI Group (UK) Ltd,
Croydon, CR0 4YY

Library of Congress Control Number: 2015930822

British Library Cataloguing in Publication data

A catalogue record for this book is available from
the British Library

MIX
Paper from
responsible sources
FSC
www.fsc.org   FSC® C013604

ISBN 978-1-84920-079-0
ISBN 978-1-84920-080-6 (pbk)

At SAGE we take sustainability seriously. Most of our products are printed in the UK using FSC papers and boards.
When we print overseas we ensure sustainable papers are used as measured by the Egmont grading system.
We undertake an annual audit to monitor our sustainability.

To Peggy and Emilia
loving companions of my personal migration

contents

preface

This volume in the *Compact Criminology* series is dedicated to a classic theme in the history of criminology, and indeed in the history of the sociological tradition – the question of migration. Beyond being a truly classic sociological theme, the issue of migration is also a well-established theme in the history of criminology and one that particularly lends itself to discussion of some of the central cores of criminological debate. In this, it is quite similar to other crucial axes of social categorization, such as gender, social class, race. Indeed it has deep interconnections with all these dimensions of sociality. And as with any of them, it quickly brings the researcher towards a basic discussion that is constitutive of any sociological criminology worth its name – indeed, the absence of any such reasoning is synonymous with a very poor (and misleading) sociology indeed. That is, it lends itself to asking the question, are the processes of criminalization directed toward those who are socially described as migrants, the result of criminal behaviour enacted by the migrants, or the result of social processes that end up targeting migrants more intensely than other groups? And, even if we were to come to the conclusion that those very processes of criminalization are indeed the result of migrants' behaviour, are there social processes that expose migrants to a higher danger of falling into that kind of behaviour?

As we shall see, these questions have not been asked always with the same degree of urgency. Sometimes they have been all but forgotten, according to the degree of attention that has been paid in specific historical periods and specific social circumstances to the question of migration, in public spheres of discussion and therefore also in sociologists' and criminologists' discourses. There is probably also some kind of deep-seated and not so obvious connection between the perception of issues of marginality – whether referring to migrants or poor or ethnic minorities – and the emergence of critical views of the established manner of thinking, therefore also of established criminological and sociological theories. Indeed, in the pages that follow (as well as in a book (Melossi 2008) where I have examined this more systematically in connection with the development of the criminological tradition) I attempt to show that there are oscillations in the ways in which, both in society and within criminology itself, the questions of social order and the treatment of marginality are connected.

There is no doubt that interest in the issue of migration for criminologists has dove-tailed with the interest of society itself. During periods of intense migration flows, the sociological and criminological spotlight has focused on migration. Migration – like race and ethnicity, with which it is strictly linked (but certainly not identical) – is a very good example of a broader criminological truth. In other words, that it is practically impossible to sever the study of criminal behaviour from the study of the processes that define, discover, label and punish behaviour as indeed criminal. It has been particularly unfortunate, in my opinion, that the last wave of international migration, large and long-lasting enough to compete with the one at the turn of the nineteenth and twen-tieth centuries, has happened at a time when the critical sensibility of criminological sociology, particularly strong in the 1960s and early 1970s, had been rejected within the more general cultural backlash that started in the late 1970s. A "criminology of the restoration" followed, that accompanied the emergence and growth of a moder-ate/conservative consensus, the cultural penchant of the "neo-liberal" revolution that started with the premiership of Margaret Thatcher in the United Kingdom and the presidency of Ronald Reagan in the United States.

As I will try to show in these pages, such a coincidence was not entirely by chance. The strength of criticism in the social sciences accompanies the strength of critique socially produced more generally, and it is in times when class division and con-flicts are more pronounced that these critiques are more liberally advanced. On the contrary, in periods of conservative hegemony such criticism is usually muffled. However, it just so happens that these periods are also periods when the power of social and economic elites in restructuring society is so broad and compelling that large migration movements again become a possibility (in the specific case of the last wave of globalization between the 1980s and the great crisis that started in 2008 such large migration flows were consequential to the world-wide victory of capitalism against its major competitor, the Soviet Bloc).

As a consequence of this very complex situation, it was difficult for the social sci-ences to see how the processes of criminalization of migrants were part of a more general picture. Particularly negative, and specific to the sociology of deviance, was the removal of the sensibilities linked with a so-called *labelling* approach, the radical consequence of which had culminated in David Matza's *Becoming Deviant* (1969). By the same token, such sensibilities had been crushed in the reaction of the mid-1970s, most symbolic for criminologists, the closing of the Berkeley School of Criminology, part and parcel of Ronald Reagan's unrelenting fight, as Governor of California, against radicalism at the University of California and more specifically at its flagship campus.

Likewise, the spreading of American criminology's power and prestige from the United States to Europe happened under a solid moderate hold. This gave to the European conservative establishment that was firmly in charge during the globalization wave the

intellectual and cultural instruments and tools that allowed for a reading of social conflict in Europe – most notably about the issue of migration – that was disconnected from
the study of processes of criminalization. Such a study – as I try to show in the pages
that follow – would have in fact made quite clear the political responsibilities of those
elites. This lack of awareness was probably less pronounced in the UK, where the presence of a critical sociology of deviance in the 1970s had been such that it was difficult to
overcome it totally. How much easier was it for such nonchalance to take hold where the
sociological tradition in deviance studies was so thin that it could not really hold against
the onslaught of governmental funds under the new agenda of "security", as happened
more or less everywhere in Continental Europe. Indeed, in the 1980s the new age of
globalization started, and with it the planetary development of the social form that Ralf
Dahrendorf (1985) had called "the society of two thirds" – a society of middle classes that
was to replace a class-divided society. The question of "security" was then reinforced by
the events of September 11 and the start of the "war on terror". It became the most prominent aspect of a set of policies where, in Loïc Wacquant's (2009: 287–314) apt metaphor,
the "right hand of the State", the penal hand, increasingly expanded at the cost of the
"left hand", the social hand.

What I shall try to make clear in this short work is that in many countries, and
on different continents, the degree of criminalization of migrants became a function
of the attitudes towards them, legally (both normatively and *de facto*), economically,
socially and culturally. Therefore, sensitivity to the issue of "labelling" – which, as
we have seen, had been unfortunately set aside – should be part and parcel of a
more capacious account of migration phenomena. It may substantially contribute to
a sociology of migration in pinpointing a crucial missing link in the relation between
structural phenomena and the "agency" of migrants.

acknowledgements

When my good friends at SAGE asked me to write this small book, I accepted enthusiastically, not only for its subject matter but also because they said they needed "only" about one hundred pages. I should have known better! The pages that follow took a long time to come and were the results of many steps in between. Among other things, I took advantage of the chance I was given to discuss some of the ideas in a number of lectures and conferences that I happened to give around the world, between 2011 and 2014. I thank all the friends and colleagues who invited me and who offered me a chance to discuss and, hopefully, improve, my ideas. Let me just thank them heartily, in no specific order: Ksenija Vidmar-Horvat, Aleksandras Dobryninas, Roberto Catanesi, Ian Loader, Carolyn Hoyle, Katja Franko Aas, Mary Bosworth, Nando Sigona, Bridget Anderson, Elena Larrauri, Gonzalo Escobar, Ignasi Bernat, Niki Lacey, Zelia Gallo, Leonidas Cheliotis, Valsamis Mitsilegas, Alessandro Spena, Karen Joe, Rossella Selmini, Malcolm Feeley, Jonathan Simon, Rosann Greenspan, José Ángel Brandariz-García, Maximo Sozzo. And their institutions: the University of Ljubljana, the University of Vilnius in Lithuania, the Italian Society of Criminology (which invited me to give a "Lectio Magistralis" on their 27th Congress), the Centre for Criminology and All Souls College at Oxford, as well as the ESRC Centre on Migration, Policy and Society at the same University, the University Pompeu Fabre of Barcelona, the University of Girona, the Centre for Criminal Justice at Queen Mary University in London (at the 2012 WG Hart Legal Workshop), the London School of Economics, the University of Palermo, the University of Hong Kong, the University of A Coruna (Spain) and last, but certainly not least, the Universidad Nacional del Litoral, Santa Fe (Argentina). I would also like to thank the friends and colleagues of the *Città sicure* Project of the Regional Government of Emilia-Romagna as well as those of the Italian journal *Studi sulla Questione Criminale*. A very special thanks goes to the Centre for the Study of Law and Society at the School of Law of the University of California at Berkeley, which hosted me on numerous occasions in these three years and gave me a chance to "rinse my language" (and my thoughts) if not in the Arno river – as a famous Italian writer wrote – at least in the Pacific Ocean! A very special thanks goes to Rubén Rumbaut for permission to reproduce Table 2.1 and to Emmanuel Saez for permission to reproduce Figure 4.1.

Another very special thanks goes to Warner Bros for the permission to use a still from the very beautiful film *America America* by Elia Kazan (1963) for the image on the cover of the book. And *grazie mille* to the Editors of this series, Niki Rafter and Paul Rock, for their wonderful support and continuous feedback! Finally, special thanks go to the Criminology Editor at SAGE, Natalie Aguilera (and her Associate Editor James Piper), Amy Jarrold and George Knowles, for their support and *patience*! Thank you all!

introduction

In the fifth edition of his famous work *Criminal Man*, Cesare Lombroso wrote, "Recent statistics for the United States [...] document high rates of crime in states with large number of immigrants, especially from Italy and Ireland. Out of 49,000 arrests in New York, 32,000 were immigrants" (Lombroso 1896–7: 316–17). As was often the case with Cesare Lombroso, his was a hotchpotch of insight and commonplace, where he succeeded in expressing the common fear and stereotypes of the public of his age under the pretence of giving them a rigorous "scientific" form. Actually, the view that associates mobility and danger is a view that goes back to the primordial period of civilization, when Greeks feared the "barbarians" who would inhabit the lands beyond their borders:

> The slave, in antiquity, is the one who comes from outside, the stranger, the barbarian: the one who has different language and customs and is therefore inferior, in a condition of servitude. Greeks thought that everybody who was not part of their world, and therefore could not speak Greek, was unable to speak, emitting merely stuttering or harsh sounds. The syllabic repetition *bar-bar*, from which the word barbarian derives, is in fact the phonetic imitation of stuttering, if not the barking of an animal (Cavalli-Sforza and Padoan 2013: 233[1]).

Much later, at the beginning of modernity, the idea of crime became associated with *vagrancy*, that "chrysalis of every species of criminal" as it would have been called at the end of the nineteenth century (Duncan 1996: 172). A veritable short circuit has always been established in people's common sense, between social change, mobility and some kind of fear or danger. In one of the most famous statements about the concept of "the stranger", by one of sociology's pioneers, Georg Simmel, the stranger is the one whose "position within [the group] is fundamentally affected by the fact that he does not belong in it initially and that he brings qualities into it that are not, and cannot be, indigenous to it" (Simmel 1908: 143). In a sense, the stranger graphically represents the discomfort and the anxiety-ridden condition of

---

[1]My translation.

social change, the danger that we more or less consciously associate with the very notion of change.

Such, however, is not the case, or is not the case to the same extent, in every period. We get accustomed in fact to what we perceive as long periods of no change, of "things as they are and should be", of peace, order and tranquillity, untouched by the dangers of change. However, alas, these are usually periods that nourish change in their womb and, when the new creature finally comes to be born, we have to face the hard labour of a new order rising (of course, not all social classes and dispositions will consider the new order alike). The sociology of migration seems therefore to me to concern the two-way relationship between a changing social structure and the movements of human beings belonging in that structure. It is probably possible to devise patterns and regularities in social change that connect to human mobility. Were this to be the case, it would also be possible to establish connections between change in social structure and the rising representations of the dangers and anxieties elicited by the sudden emergence of human mobility.

If we follow Durkheim in defining "crime" as that behaviour that society actually punishes (1893, 1895), then a good place to start could be Georg Rusche and Otto Kirchheimer's *Punishment and Social Structure* (1939), the pioneering work about relationships of social structure to punishment. Albeit criticizable on many counts, this work, developed some seventy-five years ago, represented a valiant effort to contribute to the study of the connections between changing social structure and changing punishment. Rusche's main idea[2] was that punishment is somehow related to the situation of the labour market, a situation that is in turn connected with the overall socio-economic conditions in a given society. During periods of expansion, the demand for labour increases and so do wages and the quality of work conditions. In those periods, it is likely that the social conditions related to punishment (since the modern age, in particular, detention) will improve and that imprisonment rates will decline – as those working in the tradition of Rusche and Kirchheimer started to hypothesize in the 1970s (Jankovic 1977; Greenberg 1977; Box and Hale 1982; Melossi 1985). The opposite will happen under conditions of economic difficulties, recession or even depression, when imprisonment standards will deteriorate rapidly and the numbers of people under detention will increase.

Even from such a hastily sketched reconstruction, it is apparent that a consideration of migration movements is missing. After all, Rusche and Kirchheimer wrote at the end of a period that saw an increasing importance, in Europe, of national states. Theirs is not a global or anyway international perspective, in spite of the fact that migration

---

[2]Rusche was the main inspiration behind a work that Kirchheimer was essentially called to complete (Melossi 2003b).

movements have been extremely important in Europe between the nineteenth century and the early decades of the twentieth century. In fact, the only mention of the issue of migratory movements in Rusche and Kirchheimer's work refers to the strong pro-immigration policies that characterized the period of Central European mercantilism, between the seventeenth and eighteenth centuries (Rusche and Kirchheimer 1939: 31). In that period, the strong "populationist" policies of those governments, preoccupied with the rarefaction of labour, translated into severe restrictions on e-migration and all kinds of encouragement for im-migration, especially of skilled workers. At the same time, mercantilism was the period that also marked the "discovery" of the most important antecedents of modern penal institutions, the workhouse, especially in the Netherlands, England, and Northern Germany (Rusche and Kirchheimer 1939: 41–52; Melossi and Pavarini 1977: 11–62; see Chapter One below). As we shall see, the workhouse was a type of institution geared toward preserving and reintegrating a very precious workforce that should not have been dissipated in laziness and vices but that should instead be harnessed. Contrary to what is often surmised, especially in modern times, the prison institution was at first conceived as deeply inclusive and integrating.[3]

What does it mean, however, to look for connections among the social structure, migrations, crime and imprisonment rates? According to Karl Marx, one of the first to see such connections, the vagaries of capitalist economy, crime, migration and imprisonment all relate to the historical importance of mobility for the development of modern penality. These connections have remained to a large extent unacknowledged in criminology's historical perspective, with the exception of a famous, trail-blazing, article by William Chambliss (1964), our own *The Prison and the Factory* more than a decade later (Melossi and Pavarini 1977), and Leanne Weber and Ben Bowling's 2008 essay on "valiant beggars and global vagabonds". However, the integration and inclusion of a working class that is in the process of being constructed, a working class *in fieri*, so to speak, always needs careful and attentive work. It is not that in one case, economic expansion, there is no imprisonment and in the other, economic contraction, there is. Rather, imprisonment seems to be a constant for the marginal sectors and layers of society, the outsiders, the newcomers. What seems to be changing instead is the social rational for imprisonment: to control and discipline a workforce that has become too arrogant in periods of economic expansion, to control and corral, so to speak, a mass of destitute poor who do not have any other recourse, during depressions.

---

[3]It would be too rushed to think that emigration is simply connected to recessionary periods and depression, also because where there is e-migration there is also, in another country, im-migration. So the issue would perhaps be one of world-wide economic cycles, of the kind explored by such authors as Wallerstein (1974) and Arrighi (1994).

From this particular perspective, it is not of paramount importance what kind of migrants we are talking about. In some situations, migrants are "internal" migrants, who have the same nationality as other workers (but, as we will see, their entitlements may vary a great deal!) whereas, at other times, migrants are "external" migrants, people who do not have the same nationality as other workers. Whereas today we are accustomed to thinking that these different situations may be related to different rights entitlements – greater in the case of citizenship than when this is lacking – this is not the whole story at all, because there may be situations when such is not the case. For instance, workers from member-states of the European Union (EU) today probably enjoy fuller rights than Southern Italians moving to Northern Italy forty years ago, and certainly much greater rights than workers moving around Europe in the seventeenth-century or Chinese workers without the right of residence (*hukou*) in contemporary China. As we shall see, the question of citizenship criss-crosses with the general level of labour rights, as well as other ascriptive features such as gender, age and ethnicity. As Calavita (2005) pointed out a few years ago in one of the best analyses of these matters, based on her study of the contemporary Southern European situation, the issue of criminalization is strictly related to those of "inferiorization" and "racialization".

ONE

crime and migration, development of a relationship

As I mentioned in the introduction, a comparative, and historical, perspective on the relationship between crime, punishment and migration shows that the processes of criminalization of migrants are connected, to a large extent, to the norms and practices of the countries where they are admitted. In fact, countries historically based in immigration show less crime by immigrants and less punishment of immigrants. Indeed, it is very hard to separate the human experience of mobility from definitions and labels of crime. The very fact of social change may be somehow connected, within stable, conservative societies, to notions of crime. Innovating is, in these societies, akin to crime – as Merton (1938) was to point out in one of the most deservingly famous insights of sociological criminology. And innovation may be of many different kinds but a prominent one is certainly mobility, leaving the place where one was born. In this sense, the affinity of capitalism to crime is profound, and this not only in the more traditional sense – immortalized by Proudhon (1840) – that "property is theft" (an obvious reality every time it is necessary to parcel out what was before shared possession, as ancient times, but also not so ancient times, have repeatedly demonstrated). The affinity of capitalism to crime is the outcome more generally of capitalism's penchant for social change, for stimulating, causing and propagating social change. There is no doubt that the most obvious form of social change is mobility, a mobility that will be higher, more pronounced and stronger at the time when the propulsive strength of capitalism will be particularly heightened. In this first chapter we shall therefore look, in bold sketches, at the connection between the original development of capitalism, social change, crime and punishment, up to the first wave of globalization – the one that developed in the Western world between the end of the nineteenth century and the beginning of the twentieth century.

Between the seventeenth and the eighteenth century: a pre-history

Processes of migration and "modernization" in connection with some form of "globalization", go back at least to the late Middle Ages (Wallerstein 1974). Migratory movements constituted in a sense the womb within which all types of working class originated. At first there were "people on the move" from a rural to an urban environment. At the same time, however, such a "move" was indissolubly linked with "crime" and "punishment" from the very beginning. Writing about those "enclosures of common land" in fifteenth-century England that were at the very roots of a "primitive accumulation" constitutive of a "capitalist mode of production", Marx commented:

> The proletariat created by the breaking up of the bands of feudal retainers and by the forcible expropriation of the people from the soil, this "free" proletariat could not possibly be absorbed by the nascent manufactures as fast as it was thrown upon the world. On the other hand, these men, suddenly dragged from their wonted mode of life, could not as suddenly adapt themselves to the discipline of their new condition. They were turned *en masse* into beggars, robbers, vagabonds, partly from inclination, in most cases from stress of circumstances. Hence at the end of the 15th century and during the whole of the 16th century, throughout Western Europe a bloody legislation against vagabondage. The fathers of the present working class were chastised for their enforced transformation into vagabonds and paupers. Legislation treated them as "voluntary" criminals, and assumed that it depended on their own good will to go on working under the old conditions that no longer existed. (Marx 1867: 734)

Those "dragged from their wonted mode of life", the migrants, were labelled as "criminals". Migrants are the "fathers [and mothers!] of the present working class". This is not an observation we are inclined to make during periods that are not characterized by huge mass migration, whereas it is somewhat obvious in periods like the current one. Marx further notices that "legislation treated them as 'voluntary' criminals, and assumed that it depended on their own good will to go on working under the old conditions that no longer existed". The processes that they have to undergo and that are largely brought down on them are interpreted as instances of the migrants'/vagrants' lack of adaptation or even of their predisposition to bad behaviour. The largely "involuntary" products of development are at once the culprits of their new status.

In the same way in which migrants and workers are twin modern concepts, so the destiny that was waiting for them at the end of their travel, after that "bloody [but pointless] legislation against vagabondage", was the "factory form" which doubled up as a penal factory – the *"work-house"* – which, "invented" in the sixteenth and seventeenth centuries, was both a form of relief for unemployed workers and a form of punishment for criminalized despondent workers (Melossi and Pavarini 1977: 16–33). Between the end of the sixteenth and the seventeenth century, in fact, the Amsterdam merchants literally "invented" what would then become the future "form" of the prison (but also, at the same time, of the place of manufacture, the proto-factory), the *Rasphuis*, to the end of punishing and teaching to labour at the same time (Sellin 1944). "Penality", in the English version of the "bridewell" (from the Bridewell Palace in London where it first developed), as in Dutch seventeenth-century institutions, was at the very core of the constitution of a "capitalist" mode of production; it was at the centre of the "making" of a "disciplined" "working class". At the same time, however, this very project was at the service of a certain kind of *rationality*, which was to reform and transform all aspects of social life – morality as well as work.

This overall project related very specifically to migration because what we perceive as "migration" may be defined as tantamount to a plan of anthropological transformation. In moving from one geographical, social, economic and cultural setting to a new one, the migrant is asked to change, transform himself or herself, become a "new man", and this is essentially also the implicit and sometimes explicit message of modern punishment, incorporated mostly within the prison institution. This is the essential meaning of the concept of "rehabilitation", which in my opinion represents the long-lasting ideology of imprisonment. Rehabilitation does not mean to go back to something one once had but lost – even if something of the kind may sometimes happen! – it is rather to acquire something new, a "new nature" that adjusts and adapts the human being to a new setting. There is in fact a deep craving for change and idealism in all penal projects, which makes them loved by Utopian idealists, both reformers and revolutionaries. If the prison, for instance, was the very embodiment of the project of modernity and enlightenment (Foucault 1975; Horkheimer and Adorno 1944: 225–9) and was from the very beginning "its own remedy", as Foucault writes (1975: 268), so the overcoming of imprisonment – probation – is the penal Utopia of the first half of the twentieth century. Perhaps even prison "abolitionism"[1] encloses a Utopia of social control, if what it promises is a new style of control. In this sense, a certain way of thinking about imprisonment is an indicator of the historical change that was taking place at the dawn of modernity as coherent and as telling as the introduction of the factory, the market and all the other accoutrements of capitalism; basically the same institution with a different motivation, according to the moral worth of the entering subject. Prisons – as the successors to workhouses,

---

[1] The notion that would be advisable to give up on imprisonment as a form of punishment – or, more generally, as a form of reaction to crime – altogether.

from which they were originally inspired[2] – were and are a sort of symbolic "gateway" through which the "newcomers" are "processed" in order to be admitted into the social contract, that is to say, into the "city".

In one of the central narratives of modernization, in fact, that most celebrated section of the *Manifesto of the Communist Party*, entitled "Bourgeois and Proletarians" (Marx and Engels 1848), Marx portrays the trajectory of capitalism in history as one of destruction and rebuilding (Berman 1982: 87–129). The bourgeoisie is the most revolutionary force ever to have appeared on the horizon of history (its putative grave-digger, the proletariat, had yet to show what Marx believed it could do). Marx and Engels' fascination with the "revolutionary function" of the bourgeoisie can hardly be missed:

> Constant revolutionizing of production, uninterrupted disturbance of all social conditions, everlasting uncertainty and agitation distinguish the bourgeois epoch from all earlier ones. All fixed, fast-frozen relations, with their train of ancient and venerable prejudices and opinions are swept away, all new-formed ones become antiquated before they can ossify. *All that is solid melts into air*, all that is holy is profaned, and man is at last compelled to face with sober senses his real conditions of life, and his relations with his kind. (Marx and Engels 1848: 83; Berman 1982: 95)

This "destructive nihilism" (Berman 1982: 100) is embedded in the ordinary working of capitalism (Polanyi 1944). As sociologists between the end of the nineteenth century and the first half of the twentieth century will soon realize, one of capitalism's most characteristic markers is migration and its connected coupling with a condition of "anomie" or "alienation". At the same time, these human forces that have been somehow "liberated" and set in motion by the movements of capitalism had to be transformed into production, controlled and disciplined (Hirschman 1977: 14–20) – discipline being what the factory and the prison had in common. Also, one could venture to say, Foucault's (1975) Marxian point of departure. The particular role historically played by "vagrancy", and vagrancy laws, in the very constitution of modern penal law then becomes clearer (Chambliss 1964). Vagrancy was, together with the "crime" of refusing to work at given conditions, the original crime for which imprisonment, the modern form of punishment, was to be administered (Melossi and Pavarini 1977: 16–33).

Vagrants were not only the fathers and mothers of the modern working class. Even more than that, they were the representation of a myth of the origins of the working

---

[2]William Penn's penal reform in 1681, part of the broader Quaker "holy experiment" of Pennsylvania, was the clearest and most explicit link between workhouses and modern penitentiaries. Penn decreed that, "all Prisons shall be workhouses for felons, Thiefs, vagrants, and Loose, abusive, and Idle persons, whereof one shall be in every county" (Dumm 1987: 79).

class, that was to reappear in the history of capitalism every time its destructive force would once again "sweep away" "all fixed, fast-frozen relationships", among which, the "holiest" of them all perhaps, the relationship of whole populations to "their" land. Children, men and women would then again be "on the move" (Anderson 1940), often at the same time feeling pushed and eager to go, swearing their old country,[3] full of fear and expectation for what was to come. They were damned by their former and future countrymen at the same time. Labelled as traitors because they were abandoning their land, they were then labelled as "dangerous" thieves and bandits in the cities where they took refuge, be these the "Boca" of Buenos Aires, or the Little Italies of New York or Chicago (Teti 1993).

The age of the crowd in Europe

The process outlined by Marx in the first volume of *Capital* as the very foundation of the new capitalist order would seem to indefinitely repeat itself, as a process of on-going transmigration of (potential) workers from the rural areas of the countryside to urban areas. What has been changing in the course of centuries has been – as Anthony Giddens has described it (1984) – a sort of time and space compression due to the pace of modernization. If the Free Commune of Bologna abolished the institution of serfdom in 1257 and, by so doing, produced a "surplus" of population in its countryside that started pouring into the city, walking the ten, twenty or thirty miles that separated them from the city walls, today a very similar socio-economic process is happening on the wings of jets that may carry former Chinese or African or Latin American peasants to Bologna by travelling thousands of miles. However, the overall process is remarkably similar. Whereas we may think that a major difference may reside in the fact that we look upon Chinese or African or Andean peasants as more "different" from us than we thought people from Baricella or San Giovanni in Persiceto would be, I think we do not sufficiently consider how deep were, in those days, the distinctions between town and town, small hamlet and small hamlet (so different in fact that a deep trace was left in language, given that still today somebody born in Bologna can tell from the accent that they are talking to a "stranger", born and grown up in Modena, twenty miles away!).

---

[3]As Emilio Sereni wrote in the concluding remarks of his classic *Il capitalismo nelle campagne*, the Northern Italian peasants obliged to leave their land at the end of the nineteenth century would swear, *"Porca Italia – i bastiema – andemo via"* (Sereni 1948: 414).

In the nineteenth century in Europe (but very similar processes are taking place at this very moment in China) such internal mass migrations brought about the formation of what were seen as the *"classes dangereuses"*, the *canaille sans phrase* of the nineteenth century (Chevalier 1958). This was the period of pioneering industrialization when even women and children were employed en masse in "Satan's mills", and Karl Marx's good friend and comrade Friedrich Engels (1845) could write one of the very first sociological tracts of modernity when he described the masses of workers huddled in the filthy, overcrowded and unsanitary quarters of his Manchester! Soon, as we know, the poor Irish men and women who were leaving their land after the potato famine started seeking solace from their condition, not only going eastward but also westward across the Atlantic, in a process that during the second half of the nineteenth century would bring millions of Irish people to the United States.

In the last few decades of the nineteenth century and in the period just before World War I, however, two different processes started unravelling in Europe, reinforcing each other. On the one hand, the enormous "surplus population" caused by an "industrial revolution" that swept, one after the other, across all European countries, found an outflow in emigration toward Northern and Southern America (especially the largest countries of Southern America, such as Argentina and Brazil). On the other hand, however, the conditions of the working class started to improve markedly and, together with such conditions, eventually the working class' capacity for organizing and therefore for attaining basic rights (about the length of the working day, the limitations to women's and children's work and so on) also started to improve. All throughout Europe, in country after country, first the emigration process and then the betterment in material and legal-political conditions had their repercussions on an improved feeling of security and a lightening up of criminalization processes, something that was significantly expressed in the decreasing prison populations of many countries. So, for instance, Italian criminologist Enrico Ferri, the most eminent disciple of Lombroso but one who had increasingly veered the interests of the Positive School toward sociology, noted in his *Criminal Sociology* (1884a: 93) that the decrease in the crime rates and imprisonment, first in Ireland and then, after 1881, also in Italy, was to be attributed to emigration. Emigration should therefore be listed among those tools of crime prevention that he called "penal substitutes", those methods of indirect social defence from crime that, according to Ferri, in the long run should have replaced punishment as means of crime prevention (Ferri 1884b: 334–3). This seems to be borne out in Figure 1.1, where the data of Italian imprisonment admissions appear inversely related to data on emigration from Italy, especially during the main emigration periods, at the beginning of the twentieth century and after World War II.

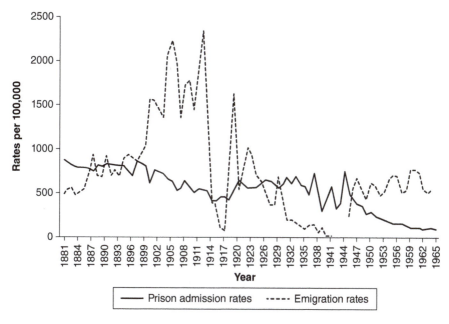

Figure 1.1 Prison admission rates and emigration rates in Italy (1881–1965) per 100,000 (My elaboration from ISTAT data)

In a later article where he reconstructed the "decreasing prison population of England" between 1857 and 1930, foremost twentieth-century American criminologist Edwin Sutherland concluded that this was not "a direct result of a reduction in the general crime rate, but rather of changes in penal policies" (1934: 200), such as the shortening of prison terms and the introduction of probation. He also noted however that "a constant or a decreasing crime rate facilitates the substitution of other measures for imprisonment, because of the feeling of security engendered by a rate of that nature" (1934: 221), the "underlying factors" for which processes were, however, "improvements in education and economic conditions" (p. 221). There is no doubt that emigration had also contributed to the change in the overall picture.

However, if the connection seemed to be established between emigration, general betterment of social conditions especially among the poorest strata of the population, and decrease of crime and imprisonment rates, the other face of the same coin seemed to be represented by Cesare Lombroso's notation, in the passage already mentioned in the introduction, according to which, "Immigrants belong to the human category with the greatest incentives and fewest barriers to committing crime. Compared to the resident population, newcomers have greater economic need, better developed jargon, and less shame; submitted to less surveillance, they more easily escape arrest. Thieves are almost always nomads" (Lombroso 1896–7: 316–17). Was this indeed the case? Beyond Lombroso's volatile, temperamental, and absolutely non-politically correct attitude, his was not an isolated position. How was the whole network of relationships between migratory movements and processes of criminalization taking shape across the ocean, in the first country where, at the same time, large-scale migratory processes were happening together with the early development of a social science deeply interested in "explaining" crime and delinquency?

Crime and migration in Chicago: an ecological theory

Between the 1880s and World War I, the United States moved from being mostly a rural country to becoming the most powerful industrial society in the world. Of course, together with massive processes of industrialization and urbanization, also huge immigration movements developed, first from Northern European countries, such as Germany and Ireland, later on from Eastern and Southern Europe, Asia and Central America (Simes and Waters 2014: 460). It would be hard to overestimate the importance of these overall processes. Emigration was often seen as a form of liberation from social, cultural and political hierarchies that the migrants considered unjust, besides being very ineffective economically. Often the migratory process would take place in two steps – something that has lasted to this very day. At first the "supernumerary" peasants would move from the countryside to the big cities, especially the major ports. Then, from there, they would migrate. And, with them, fear would migrate (Salvatore and Aguirre 1996). Southern Italians, however, were not the only ones. Russian Jews and various Eastern European peoples came too, replacing the Irish and the Germans who had crowded the Eastern seaboard ports earlier on.

The factories, stockyards and privileged logistic position of Chicago represented a big draw and, if the city was certainly not the first American urban conglomerate where the issue of crime and migration emerged as a major urban problem, neither were the specific national origins of the Chicago immigrants – Italian, Polish, Jewish, later on American Blacks from the South – the first to which a label of crime and deviance was successfully attached. All throughout the nineteenth century, the major urban centres of the East Coast had been sites of organized violence between the established groups and the newly arrived. In *The Gangs of New York* (Asbury 1928) the opposition was one, typical of the city of New York in those days, between the old established English groups and the newly arrived Irish immigrants, an opposition that replicated the one already developed in the British Isles and that was very soon connected with a form of political competition that found it rather difficult to move from the streets to the suites, so to speak.

At first, at the beginning of the twentieth century, a deep preoccupation about the pathology of migrations was linked to nativism and racism, as well as fear for the competition of migrant workers on the labour market. These fears certainly played a massive role in promoting foreigners' criminalization in the United States during the 1920s and 1930s. Whether this had to do with alcohol in the period of Prohibition or later on with drugs, such fears were strictly related to deviant representations of "non-American" peoples and habits, such as the consumption of alcohol for the Irish, of wine for Southern Europeans, of "coke" for "the Negro" or of "weed" for Mexicans (Gusfield 1963; Rainerman and Levine 1997; Knepper 2014). Soon enough, though, the sociological progressivism of the time was quick to note, against the sensationalism of the press, that immigrants' involvement in crime was not significantly higher than the natives'. Already the Immigration Commission (1911) had pointed out that the "foreign born" were less criminal than the native, a finding repeated in the Report of the Wickersam Commission (1931) (Kirk et al. 2011).

It was then the time for the first, and most genuinely American, school of sociology, the Chicago School, to produce a more sophisticated account of the relationship between migration and crime (Park 1928; Park et al. 1925; Shaw and McKay 1942; Bursik 2006). According to such accounts, migrants' criminal behaviour was the result of a "social disorganization" that was not specific to immigrant groups but had to do with the very process of migrating and thereafter of assimilating into American society. In fact, the new Chicago Department of Sociology founded, together with the rest of the university, in 1890 by John D. Rockefeller, centred its research programme around the issue of migration, an issue that was becoming at the same time a big draw for political conflict and organization, conflicts where often some of the Chicago social scientists found themselves actively engaged (they themselves were often outsiders, if not migrants or descendants of migrants). The leading experiment of the settlement movement in the United States was founded and flourished in Chicago, Jane Addams' Hull House, a vital centre for some of the Chicago leading figures of the time, from John Dewey and George Herbert Mead to William I. Thomas (Addams 1910; Bulmer 1984; Deegan 1988; Lindner 1990; Glowacki and Hendry 2004; Knight 2005). Migrations and deviance were to be seen as part and parcel of North American society and as an exemplary instance of the more general socialization process in which they were so interested. At the same time, however, the Chicago sociologists saw the social process of migration as producing conditions of unbalance and crisis, and the ambiguities of the "marginal man", the man who is at a border line among cultures (Park 1928: 205–6; Stonequist 1937).

Chicago sociologists' attitude of *appreciation* found its origin in their feelings of political and moral solidarity with the immigrants (and the other images of deviance that often overlapped with them, the hobos, the taxi-dancers, the prostitutes, the juvenile delinquents), or even in the researchers having shared at least part of their subjects' experiences. This was particularly the case with immigration, as for second generation Thorsten Sellin, the criminologist, or Nels Anderson, the author of the landmark study *The Hobo* (1923), who had been a (second generation) hobo himself, or William Isaac Thomas, the author of *The Polish Peasant* (Thomas and Znaniecki 1918–20), written together with Polish sociologist Florian Znaniecki (Cappetti 1993: 73–107).

There was, however, also a specific political reason to be fearful of migrants in those years in America. The Russian revolution had just taken place and the trustworthiness of immigrants was a particularly hot political issue. Anarchists were particularly feared, as the execution of the two Italian anarchists Nicola Sacco and Bartolomeo Vanzetti in Massachusetts in 1927 would have amply dramatized. A criminologist, Arthur MacDonald (1911), had written on political murder, inspired by the work of Cesare Lombroso with Rodolfo Laschi (Lombroso and Laschi 1890; Ruggiero 2006; Knepper 2014: 493–7). In 1919, A. Mitchell Palmer, appointed by Woodrow Wilson as his attorney-general, hired an ambitious young man, John Edgar Hoover, as a special assistant. Together they launched a campaign against radicals and left-wing organizations. On November 7, 1919 (the second anniversary of the Russian revolution!), they had over 10,000 suspected Communists and anarchists rounded up. Many were then held without trial for a long time. The vast majority were eventually released but Emma Goldman, the famous Russian-born Jewish anarchist and feminist organizer and thinker, and many others, were deported to Russia. On 2 January 1920, another 6,000 were arrested and held without trial, many of them members of the Industrial Workers of the World.[4] In these "Palmer raids", which took place in several cities, the young J. Edgar Hoover gained his early experience as police organizer and spymaster and in 1924 became director of the Bureau of Investigation (then renamed the FBI in 1935).

The cultural and political climate at Chicago, in those very years, meant also that the notion of "social control" – which was at the centre of the Chicagoans' research program – had meanings and nuances that were quite different from those that would later become canonical after Parsons' revisitation of Durkheim in the middle of last century (Melossi 1990: 132-9). Robert E. Park and Ernest W. Burgess proclaimed social control to be "the central problem of society" (1921: 42). So, for instance, Park addressed the issue of "the problem" of the "immigrant press" and "its control" in a research report that he wrote at the time (Park 1922). The problem of the immigrant press was linked to fear of foreign criminal organizations (for instance around the

---

[4]The IWW, also known as "the Wobblies", founded in Chicago in 1905, was an all-American working-class organization preaching the unity of all industrial workers beyond differences of trade, nationality, or race, characterized by notions of industrial struggle emphasizing organization and a pragmatic notion of radicalism.

issue of trafficking of "white slave" women [Knepper 2014: 489–93]), but especially to fear for their supposedly radical political leanings. Contrary however to the thrust of the "Palmer raids", Park, in the conclusion of his essay, and in a manner quite characteristic of the Chicago perspective, stated that the only way to overcome ethnic or political barriers was to foster the development of immigrant discourse toward a more universalistic conceptual and linguistic vocabulary. According to the prevailing Pragmatic ethos in Chicago, as this had been formulated by the likes of William James

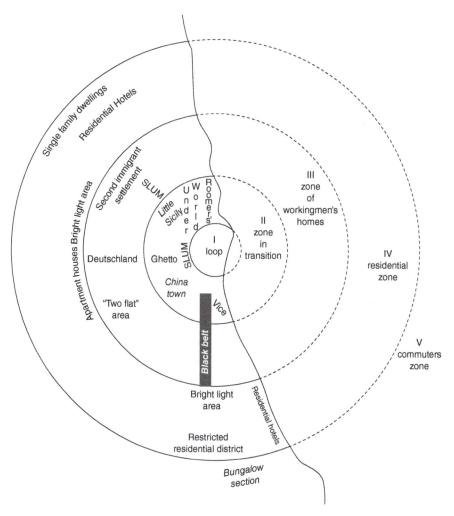

Figure 1.2 Map of the urban areas of Chicago according to the Chicago School (Park et al. 1925: 55)

(1907) and George Herbert Mead (1925, 1934), social control was seen not as the result of "state" censorship and repression – which would certainly not disappear but should lie in the background – but as the outcome of a consensus formation resulting from "competition" in the arena of free speech. This was to be the proper terrain of *social control*. Competition among the diverse vocabularies of the many native languages of the immigrants, as well as of the many political vernaculars, would be analysed and treated, by the social scientist, as instances of limited worlds. The objective would then be the promotion of linguistic, cultural and political integration into the larger universe of American society – an integration that was to crucially complement the economic integration resting on the actual technological insertion of the immigrant worker into the productive process (Melossi 1990: 118–21).

The central inspiration of the Chicago School authors was in fact a kind of cultural, in the sense of *ecological*, determinism. According to them, the socio-cultural environment, and especially the neighbourhood, where a group, and the individual in a group, grows up and dwells, carries the kind of behaviour that will eventually tend to prevail (for a present-day version of this view see Sampson 2012). The map that we can see in Figure 1.2 – probably the most famous map in the history of sociology – represents Chicago sliced in concentric semicircles, from the innermost one, the Loop, the business district, to the outermost, the suburban area. With the development of the city, both the immigrant dwelling and the shadiest activities became increasingly crowded near the Loop, in what the Chicago sociologists called a "zone in transition". This was also at the same time, however, the entry point for first generation migrants. If there is a connection between migration and crime, the Chicago sociologists seem to suggest, it is therefore because of the structural position in which migrants find themselves, a social structural position which is at the same time also an ecological location – in a place where primary social controls are by definition at the lowest point. Clifford Shaw and Henry D. McKay in particular established a relationship between the spatial structure of the city, the immigrant population settlements and indicators of the various "social pathologies", such as the crime rate (Shaw and McKay 1942) and the rate of mental illness (Farris and Dunham 1934). The newly arrived immigrants in this core area showed in fact a higher degree of social pathology because they resided in an environment where social mobility, heterogeneity and "anonymous" relationships were much higher. Shaw and McKay advanced therefore the idea of *social disorganization*, the notion, that is, that, according to such an "ecological" hypothesis, the various types of deviance did not derive from qualities pertaining to single individuals, but were rather qualities of the socio-cultural environment where they resided. Social disorganization was caused by the coming apart of social control, in particular the kind of social control that Chicagoans deemed so important, *primary* social control, i.e. the one depending on "natural", direct, intimate relationships among individuals. The social mobility, heterogeneity and anonymity of "transitional" zones meant that lasting ties among individuals could not be built. Not knowing each other, they did not care for each other and neither would they care about what other people thought of them. There was no system of mutual expectations, no control through the gaze of the neighbour, or of the passer-by. Often they did not even have ways to communicate with each other. There was no "reference group" to speak of – as this view would be formulated later on (Shibutani 1962). Migration, in other words, may be linked to crime not because of something having to do with the individual "inclination" of migrants but because the experience of migration exposes migrants to higher risk (Davies and Fagan 2012).

In particular, the first generation of immigrants, in fact, especially if they were young single males, as they often were, seemed to be taken between the "social disorganization" of the first settlement areas, and the types of orientations they carried within themselves, so to speak, from their original culture. Such orientation was particularly reinforced when they managed to move to the ethnic enclaves where they "belonged". However, as soon as they, and especially their offspring, "integrated" within a more established area of Chicago, they started adjusting to the type of cultural influence that was specific to that area, and that even different immigrant groups would transmit to one another. Chicagoans were therefore characteristically ambivalent on the issue of whether there are criminological reasons to assume that immigrants may become more involved in crime than non-immigrants ("citizens"). On the one hand, the school posited a "social disorganization" condition, especially for the "transitional areas", that ought to be related to a higher incidence of crime because of the drastic reduction of social controls (such reduction may be compensated by an increase in formal social control, policing and so on – a possibility however on which the neo-Chicagoan "labelling" approach of the 1960s will cast a doubtful light!). Immigration *per se*, however, will have an effect on the first generation only insofar as it entails the reproduction of the crime customs of the origins. Therefore crime will be higher or lower according to the situation in the native country.

Such a situation of anomie – that nineteenth-century European criminologists traditionally had started to associate with the great city, the metropolis, and with immigration into the great city from the surrounding countryside areas – was, however, limited to the very early immigration by new groups, when typically young men come by themselves and locate into the new society. Given however that the experience of "social disorganization" is not a very rewarding one, not even for young males, usually they tried, after a while, to move on to the circle farther out, where people like themselves had settled several years before. Therefore, this initial situation typically lasted a short time, soon to be replaced with migration chains where new immigrants came in contact with previous immigrants from their country and often from their region, locality or even family. When the immigrant arrived into the new country, he or she found a set of conditions that were already quite structured, and forms of social control often more rigid and stricter than either in the country of origin or in the general population of the country of destination. At the same time, one should also note that often it was precisely the hope of escaping the strict controls of the culture of the small town, and/or of the old country, that brought at least some of these young men, and women, to migrate. Indeed the case of women acquired a very specific salience in Chicago, perhaps because of the truly subversive impact of life in the big city toward the rigid patriarchal nature of life in the rural atmosphere of the small town or the countryside. As Thomas and Znaniecki will write (see p. 22), "[we] have here, of course, only one specification of the unrest which characterizes America and American women" (Thomas and Znaniecki 1918–20: 1821) or, in a literary version, consider the unforgettable portrayal of "Sister Carrie" in Theodor Dreiser's masterpiece (Dreiser 1900).[5]

This led to the formation of so-called "ethnic enclaves" such as "Little Sicily", "Deutschland" or "the Ghetto" (by which Chicagoans at the time meant the Eastern European Jewish settlement), and finally the "Black Belt". Within such enclaves one could also find all the services of the new metropolis of immigrants, often "ethnically" specialized, such as the famous "Chinese" laundries, as well as the skid-row and red-light districts, and the saloons, brothels, flophouses, the first fast food joints, the temporary employment agencies (see the magnificent description by Nels Anderson of life in the Chicago "main stem" in *The Hobo* [Anderson 1923]). Later on, during Prohibition, this was the area of "speakeasies" and their "gangsters". In these highly structured areas, contrary to the social disorganization thesis, we shall have every reason to expect higher conformity to laws and customs and it would make sense to expect a powerful anti-crime effect of social capital and family structure (Whyte 1943; Bursik 2006; Ousey and Kubrin 2009: 452; Sampson 2012: 31–49). Here "organized crime" played a very ambivalent role because it certainly maintained a tight control on an area, but of oppositional nature toward the putatively normative social control (putative because the men of the law were often "on the take" from criminal organizations [Sutherland 1937; Chambliss 1978]). This was also the reason why Edwin Sutherland would later prefer thinking in terms of "differential social organization" rather than "social disorganization" (Sutherland and Cressey 1978).

Even social disorganization could, however, become established as a neighbourhood "culture". So, for example, the area of the "Cabrini projects" in Chicago was

---

[5]On the connections between the Chicago sociology and the Chicago literature of the period see Carla Cappetti (1993).

always characterized by a very high murder rate, first when it was inhabited by Sicilians, and later when the Sicilians were replaced by African Americans. It could not be more incorrect, therefore, to hypothesize that "integration" and "crime" are at opposite poles, as it is often said. On the contrary, integration may mean integration within specific criminal traditions and activities, and may result in a higher crime rate than the one characterizing the migrant group in its culture of origin (Walklate and Evans 1999). The Chicago School sociologists observed that the various groups, moving from one circle to the next, tended to leave the cultural characteristics of the circle they were coming from and assume instead those of the circle in which they were settling – including the "proper" crime rates. The most important conclusion reached by the Chicago School, insofar as the sociology of crime is concerned, was therefore that *deviant characteristics are a property of the environment and not of given groups or individuals (such as "migrants" or "ethnic minorities").*

Second generations and "internal" migrations: between "culture conflict" and a "structural frustration" (or "anomie")

The legislative changes in immigration laws in 1924 – based also in fear of a supposed "crime threat" (Simes and Waters 2014: 459) – brought *de facto* a restriction of "undesirable" immigrants, undesirable on political and racial grounds, making it much more difficult to immigrate for Southern and Eastern Europeans, Asians and, later on, Mexicans. Such changes contributed to redefining the issue of migration and crime also for sociologists and criminologists. On the one hand, in fact, they started paying increased attention to the crimes committed by the children of immigrants, so called "second generations", caught between the old world of their parents and the new world. Theirs was a classic situation of *anomie* or "culture conflict", in the words of the sociologist Thorsten Sellin (1938). On the other hand, African Americans migrating from the Southern US states toward the great urban centres (Wilkerson 2010), started igniting the chain of events that was eventually to give rise to "the American underclass" of later debates (Wilson 1987). What is, in fact, the peculiar condition of that generation which is to be found between the first and those who will become better established later on, what we would call "second generations"? At first, socio-criminological literature would connect the condition of second generations to the malaise that is caused by the unhappy situation of the one who is "between cultures", the one who Stonequist (1937) and Park (1928) defined as "the marginal man". This essay by Park is a true paean elevated to migration as a source and creation of culture and civilization. Unsurprisingly counterposed to theorists such as Arthur de Gobineau – one of the founders of modern racism – Park compares the great migratory movements to the great social upheavals that have deeply transformed the world, such as wars, revolutions[6] and the birth of great religions "like Mohammedamism or Christianity" (Park 1928: 199). Migration is akin to social change and social innovation, and the migrant human being is in a sense the bearer of this process, of this movement that he or she brings along – a true human incorporation of Marx's idea that, with the advent of capitalism, *"all that is solid melts into air*, all that is holy is profaned, and man is at last compelled to face with sober senses, his real conditions of life, and his relations with his kind" (Marx and Engels 1848: 83; Berman 1982: 95). Park's migrant, Park's "marginal man", carries within himself, or herself, this unhappy condition that he or she shares with Georg Simmel's description of the "stranger" (Simmel was the sociologist to whom the Chicagoans felt closer, Berlin being to them the "Chicago on the Spree"). Simmel however had been inspired – Park suggests – by the condition of the "emancipated Jew", which he himself was. The condition of "the wanderer" was tantamount to that of modernity, and concepts of European marginality would become the norm of the new society that was being built in America, and especially in Chicago:

> ... a man on the margin of two cultures and two societies, which never completely interpenetrated and fused ... the city man, the man who ranges widely, lives preferably in a hotel – in short, the cosmopolite ... something of the same sense of moral dichotomy and conflict is probably characteristic of every immigrant during the period of transition, when old habits are being discarded and new ones are not yet formed. It is inevitably a period of inner turmoil and intense self-consciousness ... in the case of the marginal man the period of crisis is relatively permanent ... It is in the mind of the marginal man that the moral turmoil which new cultural contacts occasion manifests itself in the most obvious forms. It is in the mind of the marginal man – where the changes and fusions of culture are going on – that we can best study the processes of civilization and of progress. (Park 1928: 205–6)

Change, crime, and innovation are therefore strict relatives – Robert K. Merton's great intuition, as we shall see (and as Jock Young would not tire of telling us) – the difference between "crime" and "innovation" being largely the product of how society accommodates innovation, a difference that is related to the ways in which the social change signified by marginal men and women is socially labelled (something however that sociology would learn about only thirty years later, in the 1960s).

The perspective of the marginal man would then be developed by Thorsten Sellin (1938), a "second generation" himself (Melossi 2010a), under the heading of

---

[6]A few years before, a follower of Freud, Paul Federn, had made a similar point from the perspective of psychoanalytic theory, comparing the European Communist revolutions that were taking place in Europe at the time, and America as a society of migrants, both having in common the fact of being societies that "had lost the father" (Federn 1919–20; Melossi 1990: 72–91).

"the conflict of conduct norms", by distinguishing "primary culture conflicts", as those derived directly from different cultural origins, typical of the foreign born, from "secondary culture conflicts", derived instead from the "process of social differentiation" and typical of second generations (Sellin 1938: 104–5). Sellin furthermore highlights the "anomie" deriving from economic deprivation and the malaise of second generations "finding the ways of their parents despised in the larger community" (Sellin 1938: 101), given that the insertion of immigrants in the social structure of the destination country usually happens from the bottom.

There are reasons to think, however, that this may apply to those of the second generation more than to the first migrant generation. These "difficult" second generations are "culturally integrated" and "structurally excluded", in the words of British sociologist and (new-) criminologist Jock Young, trying to apply and develop further Robert K. Merton's anomie theory (Young 1999: 81; Merton 1938; Young 2003; Simes and Waters 2014: 461). According to Merton, the disadvantaged position of migrants within the legitimate opportunity structure might end up encouraging the adoption of innovative but illegitimate means to reach the social goals, also because, at the same time, illegitimate opportunity structures might be more readily available within their neighbourhoods (Cloward and Ohlin 1960; Melossi 2008: 144–9; Davies and Fagan 2012; Martinez and Slack 2013). This might apply more directly to second generation migrants because they have after all been exposed to that "promise of democracy" in which they were in fact educated, and inspired to a principle of equality.

This is particularly the case when and if the source of such discriminatory attitude extends to the police, i.e. to the very agency that ought to be in charge of enforcing those principles of equality preached within the schools that second generation children have attended. This overall type of situation may have something to do with the observation, recurring in gang research – starting with Frederic Thrasher's classic study (1927) of the 1,313 gangs that he counted in Chicago in the 1920s, all of European (or African American) descent – that often young people of the second generation are one of the favourite recruiting pools for gangs. They, as, more recently, the Dominican kids making up the ranks of David Brotherton's "street organizations" (Brotherton 2008a), perceive in a sense that they need to organize their own "self-defence", when, tired of being bullied around but being left defenceless by those with the duty to protect them (when not bullied by them too [Venkatesh 2008: 219–46]), these children and young men take it on themselves to defend their "turf" from the assaults of "outsiders". Such defence is at first from native youth groupings, but then, increasingly, from other migrants groups, or even later on from their own group but from other neighbourhoods (Anderson 1990). Not much time goes by, often, before what was at first legitimized as a defence of their own community – especially in the absence of politically conscious "vanguards" able to understand the complexity of the social processes involved – turns into organizations that are parasitical on the very communities they claim to protect, forms of mafia-style organized crime (Venkatesh 2008).

Two other Chicago authors, William I. Thomas and Florian Znaniecki, also making a very Mertonian point *ante litteram*, observed the following, in their essay on Polish immigrant "girls" in 1920s Chicago:

> Perhaps the girl would settle down unrevoltingly to … steady life, however dull, if the apparent possibilities of an entirely different life, full of excitement, pleasure, luxury and showing-off, were not continually displayed before her eyes in an American city. Shop windows, theatres, the press, street life with its display of wealth, beauty and fashion, all this forms too striking a contrast to the monotony of the prospect that awaits her if she remains a "good girl." If she felt definitely and irremediably shut off from this "high life" by practically impassable class barriers, as a peasant girl in Europe feels, she might look at all this show of luxury as upon an interesting spectacle with no dream of playing a role in it herself. *But even aside from the idea of democracy – which though it does not mean much to her politically, teaches her to think that the only social differences between people are differences of wealth* – she feels that some small part at last of this gorgeousness actually is within her reach, and her imagination pictures to her indefinite possibilities of further advance in the future. Sooner or later, of course, she will be forced back into her destined channel by society, by the state, by economic conditions, will be forcibly "reformed" and settled, not into a satisfied, positively moral course of life but to a more or less dissatisfied acceptance of the necessary practical limitations of her desires and of the more or less superficial rules of *decorum*. But before her dreams are dispelled she tries to realize them as far as she can. We have here, of course, only one specification of the unrest which characterizes America and American women. (Thomas and Znaniecki 1918–20: 1820–1, my emphasis)

Indeed, beyond such condition of "being taken between two cultures", second generations usually experience the reality of discrimination, both the discrimination that their parents had to go through and the discrimination that they themselves have to suffer, so much more present to them if they are also perceived as so-called "ethnic minorities". The contrast with the promise of democracy and equality could not be greater, and it is the source of great frustration and anger.

In 1932, when Franklin Delano Roosevelt was elected President on the basis of a "New Deal" with the American public, the notorious Alphonse Gabriel Capone – later known as Al "Scarface" Capone – had already been convicted and jailed. Born in Brooklyn, New York, on 17 January 1899, from parents who came from Naples' surrounding areas in Southern Italy, he had been the head of a gang, in Chicago, mostly made up of second generation (Southern) Italians who had prevailed on other second generation groups, especially over control of Prohibition era bootlegging operations. Al Capone and his organization had acquired more and more salience, feeding into a collective representation that proceeded together with the increasing importance of mass media of communication. The period between the 1920s and Roosevelt's New Deal was in fact also the period when public interest in crime started to develop and, together with it, both the implementation of agencies and legislation devoted to fighting crime, and the study of crime from a socio-criminological perspective. After the Depression and in the changed political climate of the New Deal, the now all-powerful master of the FBI, J. Edgar Hoover, had somewhat lost interest in "radical strangers", concentrating instead on all-American "public enemies", who were now high-profile "gangsters", such as the just-mentioned Al Capone, and also the likes of John Dillinger, or Bonnie Parker and Clyde Barrow (Burrough 2005; Gorn 2009).

In a 1953 landmark work, sociologist Daniel Bell reconstructed the development of organized crime in America as an aspect of the social climbing, and the increasing integration, of the various ethnic groups, in turn, into an "American Way of Life". Whether Italian or Irish or Jewish or Polish, according to Bell the various gang organizations grew in an increasingly deep complicity with the urban power machines. Such an unconventional power structure was then used in order to enter the conventional power structure, and the old gangsters' children, now turned lawyers, engineers or small entrepreneurs, could finally be admitted into the American middle class. When Daniel Bell was writing, in the early 1950s, this process had almost come to completion for Americans of European descent, while groups coming from other ethnic minorities, especially African Americans (who were also migrants, but *internal* migrants, coming from the South), were starting to replace ethnic Europeans in the new gang formations.

Indeed, after the introduction, in 1924, of a "quota" system to contain "undesirable" alien populations, the mass migration of African American rural workers from the South to the North, already started during World War I intensified even more (Wilkerson 2010). These workers were escaping the Jim Crow laws and the blatant racism of the post-bellum era in the South (Alexander 2012).[7] These had been developing within a general shift back to white supremacy in the old Confederate states as part of the backlash against the Civil War and the years immediately after, when a "radical" Reconstruction had been attempted. In fact, the end of the regime of legal slavery and the acquisition of at least formal rights of citizenship by the African American minority had meant the end of the "domestic" punishments inflicted by the slave master, true *pater familias*. There started that "disproportion" in the experience of (public) penality that stayed on thereafter in the African American experience. Also the Southern states saw, after the Civil War, a

---

[7] An escape narrated most famously by the first great African American writer, Richard Wright (1940, 1944).

sudden and massive increase in African American presence within prisons, similar to what had already happened in the North, where a small free section of the black population was already filling public prisons (Sabol 1989). There appeared at this point quite clearly what Thorsten Sellin (1976) called *penal slavery*.[8] As Angela Davis explains (2003), missing slave labour was therefore replaced by forced prison labour, first with the introduction, in the South, of the convict lease system, a contract system that provided a very convenient form of cheap labour to private plantations and corporations (Melossi and Pavarini 1977: 130–42; Mohler 1924–5), replacing in a sense the slave labour that had been lost (it goes without saying that the great part of prisoners who had to go through this were African Americans). The system was plagued with corruption and violence. Together with chain gangs (which have recently resurfaced in Alabama and Arizona), blacks were brought back to the plantation as convicts, submitting to the same "domestic" punishments, but this time as disciplinary punishments within the penal realm. First as "chattels", then as forced labour under contract, they were exposed to the destiny of a fully expendable life.[9]

A new phenomenological perspective

Indeed, a different kind of migrants started arriving to the shores of the United States in the 1930s. They were the refugees who were fleeing from the totalitarian and murderous regimes which had taken over most of Europe. One of these was Alfred Schutz, an Austrian Jew, who put his background in phenomenology to the service also of a self-understanding of his own, uneasy, condition in the new land. He then discovered that the attitude of the stranger and the attitude of the sociologist have something

---

[8]Developing an intuition by German theorist Gustav Radbruch (1938).

[9]Did they come close to being an example of what Giorgio Agamben has called "bare life" (1995)? The mind goes to German concentration camps during World War II or Stalin's gulags – a concept of full fungibility of labour power that is hard to detach from what Foucault has called "State racism" (1976). In 1939, in a letter to Horkheimer in New York, Georg Rusche stated that he was ready to write an article, for the journal of the Institute of Social Research, on "the most recent development of the German penal policy". These were, "the unbelievable scarcity of workers", that had caused, in Germany, "truly interesting new phenomena", among which, Rusche (who also was of Jewish ancestry) probably had in mind the emerging forced labour camps (Melossi 2003b: xxix–xxx). Years before, in 1934, while he was revising the manuscript of *Punishment and Social Structure* in London, apparently he wanted to extend his discussion to the cases of Russia and India, and also in Russia Rusche saw the determining factor in the scarcity of workforce, having as a consequence an extensive utilization of coercive labour (Lévy and Zander 1994: 16, 66).

in common, to the point that – in his famous essay "The Stranger" – the question of "translation" was identified as one of central significance to social theory, becoming a metaphor for mobility and the mediation of cultural frames of reference:

> The discovery that things in his (or her) surroundings look quite different from what he expected them to be at home is frequently the first shock to the stranger's confidence in the validity of his habitual "thinking as usual". Not only the picture which the stranger has brought along of the cultural pattern of the approached group but the whole hitherto unquestioned scheme of interpretation current within the home group becomes invalidated. It cannot be used as a scheme of orientation within the new social surroundings. For the members of the approached group their cultural pattern fulfils the functions of such a scheme. But the approaching stranger can neither use it simply as it is nor establish a general formula of transformation between both cultural patterns permitting him, so to speak, to convert all the coordinates within one scheme of orientation into those valid within the other (Schutz 1944: 503–4).

In a sense we could say that, according to Schutz, the stranger is obliged to behave as a "practical sociologist" in attempting to decode the cultural patterns of a social group that is essentially foreign to him. As we have seen, Georg Simmel (1908) had written of the stranger as the visitor who is with us to stay, somebody we can identify as foreign but who, at the same time, is remaining with us. The stranger is different from us and, implicit in this very difference, one can detect something "dangerous". As long as this traditional view is going to prevail, a traditional view that is often fanned by the racist and xenophobic discourse of the most reactionary political sectors in each country (van Dijk 1993), Abdelmalek Sayad (1999), the Algerian sociologist, will be right in stating that a "double suspicion" toward the immigrant tends to prevail. The stranger, being already at fault for his or her being a stranger, will be an easy target, a "suitable enemy", according to Nils Christie's expression (1986), for suspicion of all kinds of deviant and criminal acts. If only some stranger will actually engage in such acts – not least for the reasons that labelling theorists would have then explained so well – the vicious circle will be closed, and the stranger will suffer from a double level of guilt, for his strangeness and for his deviance, already implicit and wholly predictable in his being a stranger (see also Bauman 1997: 35–45).

Big factory, big house

Whereas in the late nineteenth century the American economy had been dominated by the production of heavy mechanical goods at the time of railways, and the central working role was that of the skilled worker, usually of German or Irish descent, in the decades that followed the new invention of the assembly line emerged and, with it, the production of the automobile and of other durable goods of mass consumption (Baran and Sweezy 1966). Henry Ford's new invention was fed by the huge mass migration of (industrially) unskilled Southern and Eastern European peasants to America. Later on, this new model of production and consumption spread, beyond the great depression of the 1930s, and well into the 1970s, from the United States throughout the Western world, thanks to the American hegemony that followed World War II. This new "Fordist" style of production – where the rationalization of factory work ("Fordism" proper) was coupled with the "scientific" management of work ("Taylorism") – was especially geared toward hiring a recent working class without industrial skills, a mass of former peasants who, by moving toward the centres of an industrial development not too demanding in terms of skills, could easily be employed and find a job. This is essentially what happened first in the United States, in relation to the war economy, and later in Europe after the war, based on the funds of the Marshall Plan. Such developments put to work an increasing number of migrants, sometimes "internal", such as the African Americans who moved from the South to the North and the West of the United States, or, in Europe, Southern European peasants who moved toward the central areas of European industrial development. Increasingly, however, after the 1970s, it was a matter of "external" migrants. How much the invention of "Fordism" – pivoting around a newly discovered technology – was a response to the availability of cheap and inexperienced labour of peasant background, and how much the assembly line attracted instead that pool of labour, is a question of the chicken and the egg. Certainly, the two went together very well (from the perspective of capitalist work organization) in the first half of the twentieth century! This would therefore suit migrants, in the United States as well as, after World War II, in Australia, Canada and Western Europe generally. To migrate had been relatively easy in the United States before the stop of 1924 and the following economic crisis. Again, it would be relatively easy in Europe immediately after the war.

If on the one hand this is therefore the period of the big factory – especially represented by the auto industry – it is also, on the other hand, the period of prison as "the big house" (Jacobs 1978), in which the connections among economic cycle, unemployment rate and imprisonment rate make good sense.[10] As Georg Rusche had

---

[10]According to King et al. (2012), US criminal deportations were connected to rates of unemployment, especially in the period between 1941 and 1986. Later on, changes in criminal deportation rates show similar trends to incarceration rates, so large that they are largely independent from economic indicators.

predicted and as the first 1970s analyses of those relationships seemed to validate, economic prosperity was to be accompanied by large penal institutions devoted to a rehabilitative ideal. Prosperity makes it easier to comply with what Rusche and Kirchheimer, deriving it from eighteenth-century social philosophers, called "the less eligibility threshold", the principle of deterrence that recommends that standard of living in prisons be always maintained at a lower level than the worst level in free life outside. All of this will soon start to change in the period of the deep crisis of the 1970s. During the long restructuring period between the 1970s and the 1990s, finally ushering in the second great wave of globalization, much of the social landscape eventually formed will look like a throwback to previous periods of unrestrained capitalist development (such as the "roaring twenties"): capitalist arrogance, increasing social inequality, deep divisions in the working class due to the new "post-Fordist" setting, massive migration flows, soaring imprisonment rates and a new culture of penal cruelty (especially in the Southern states of the US, still very much the "guiding light" of this whole development).

TWO

crime, punishment and migration in an age of globalization: America

A comparative perspective on the relationship between crime, punishment and migration shows that the processes of criminalization of migrants depend to a large extent on the situation the migrants find in the countries where they are admitted. A good example is the relationship between migration and crime in the United States, which is marked by a pattern that is essentially favourable to the experience of migration, in spite of the recurrent bouts of anti-immigrant sentiment. This is not surprising, in a country which is after all constituted on migration and even more on the *myth* of migration. At the same time, it is also a country that is premised on the centrality of social change and innovation. The main rhetoric of American capitalism is the capacity for change and innovation. Migration and innovation are the twin aspects of social change. In the more "progressive" and propulsive periods of American history they seem both to be welcome. After such periods, when a more pioneer-like and "heroic" mood yields to the need for re-establishing social order, retrenchment and resentment eventually follow.

From cultural to normative conflict: a theory of differential association

The immigration–crime nexus disappeared from the agenda of American sociologists and criminologists for a long time, during the long decades of the Depression, World War II and then post-war economic prosperity. This was due to a number of causes. These were periods when the conflicts *internal* to American society tended to prevail on what Thorsten Sellin had called "cultural conflicts", conflicts somehow "imported" into America from outside (or what seemed so). Accordingly, in criminology, interests moved from "first" to "second" generations and, together with such a move, to issues of class, race and youth – all somehow "internal" to American society. The shift, in the 1930s, from Sellin's "cultural conflict" to Sutherland's "normative conflict" would be quite indicative of such a change. As Donald Cressey (1968) would make clear in an essay for the collective volume in honour of Thorsten Sellin, one of the consequences of the stop to immigration in the 1920s, first with the quotas introduced in 1924 by the Immigration Act, then with the Great Depression in the 1930s, would be a drastic change of scenario in criminology. Attention was to shift from first generation migrants to the issue of the integration of second generations, the children of those who had made it in, therefore from the centrality of "cultural conflict", with Sellin, to that of "normative conflict", with Sutherland. According to the latter, conflict was not articulated any longer only to cultural and national differences, but, in a society where the various migrants groups had by and large mixed together, social class stratification was emerging as the most important organizing concept. What else should one have expected, on the other hand, from the sociologist who had created the concept of "white collar crime", probably the most direct heritage of Roosevelt's New Deal to criminology? In the version of Sutherland's textbook reworked by Donald R. Cressey at the end of the 1970s (the tenth and, for all practical purposes, last edition of the famous "Sutherland and Cressey"[1]), the question of "nativity" was lumped together with "race" and it was certainly "race" that attracted most attention. This concept of a "normative" and not "cultural" conflict was strongly connected to Sutherland and Cressey's more general theoretical point about "differential association theory", the idea, that is, "that high crime rates occur in societies and groups characterized by conditions that lead to the development of extensive criminalistic subcultures" (Sutherland and Cressey 1978: 95; Sutherland 1942: 20–1). Such "conditions" may however be connected to cultural transmigration of norms as well as cultural differences linked to social class or other "structural" elements. Sutherland's theory was essentially a development of Chicago's social and cultural ecology (Melossi 2008: 133–41). He moved from the Chicagoans' observation that the various generations of migrants would slowly shift from the ecological pressure of the culture of origin to the one of the receiving country (and more specifically

---

[1]Cressey having been my main mentor at the University of California, Santa Barbara, in 1979–86, I recall that by far the most impressive presence in Cressey's office (that, by the standards of UCSB's modern buildings was large, but not *very* large) was a huge bust of FDR in the centre of the windowsill, impossible to ignore. Typically, after a visitor's inevitable comment, one variant of a story followed – and Cressey was an amazing story-teller! – according to which, Cressey being of humble origins, his affection and gratitude for Roosevelt knew no limits.

of the receiving city, and neighbourhood). Contrary to the common-place idea that migrant crime may be due to "lack of integration", the perspective of differential association theory suggested to him that:

> crime among immigrants was not due to an inherent flaw or weakness plaguing the immigrant population; rather, immigrant criminality could mainly be attributed to the increased acculturation of these groups into a generally more crime-prone American society. In short, the longer immigrants resided in the United States, the more criminal they became. (Berardi and Bucerius 2014: 556–7)

What could be observed among the crime rates of the various generations of migrants was "a slow process of 'catching up' (or a social form of 'naturalization') to the baseline rate of the native-born population" (Hagan et al. 2008: 100).

Therefore, it was only with the recent "age of globalization" that North American criminological and sociological interests again turned to address the issue of migration, and this time contemporaneously to what was happening in Europe and other immigration catalysts in the world. When the epigones of the Chicago School, such as Robert Sampson, started to turn their attention to the results of globalization, they seemed to come up with outcomes not very remote from what had been the classic Chicago School and Sutherland's findings. Even very recently, in fact, Robert Sampson (2006) noted that first generations are in a sense "protected", by their relationships with their original families, within tried and true "ethnic niches", which – as W.E.B. Du Bois had already classically observed in *The Philadelphia Negro* (1899) – separate the migrant youths from the more obviously crime-prone currents of the context in which they find themselves. Sampson could even maintain – to the chagrin of his many conservative critics – that in the 1990s Mexican immigration to the United States was one of the factors contributing to declining crime rates (Karmen 2000; Sampson 2006). Indeed, if the decade of the 1990s, on the one hand, had been the decade of globalization, at the same time it had been also a decade of intense immigration, seemingly going back to the levels of a century earlier. It was, however, also a decade of declining crime rates. In the words of sociologist of migration Rubén G. Rumbaut:

> In 1970, the U.S. census had found that the foreign-born population accounted for only 4.7 percent of the total population — the lowest proportion since 1850, when it first recorded the country of birth of U.S. residents. But by 1980, the foreign-born population had grown to 14.1 million, or 6.2 percent of the national total; by 1990 it had grown to 19.8 million (7.9 percent); by 2000, to 31.1 million (11.1 percent); and it has been growing by more than one million per year since. More immigrants came in the 1980s than in any previous decade but one (1901–10, the peak years of mass migration from Europe when the foreign-born population reached 14.7 percent of the U.S. total); and more immigrants came in the 1990s than in any other decade — a total that

may be surpassed in the present decade, adding to the largest immigrant population in history (both legal and illegal). By 2008, over 70 million persons in the United States were of foreign birth or parentage (first or second generations) — about 23 percent of all Americans, including 75 percent of all "Hispanics" and 90 percent of all "Asians". Immigrants are heavily concentrated in metropolitan areas, are predominantly non-white, speak languages other than English, reflect a wide range of religious and cultural backgrounds, and arrive with a mix of legal statuses. (Rumbaut 2008: 4)

At first the migrants' cultures of origin are crime-adverse, and this is especially the case, as mentioned, within so-called "ethnic enclaves" (Sampson 2006; Martinez and Valenzuela 2006; Stowell 2007; Stowell et al. 2009). However, when their offspring integrate within American society, one of the consequences of the integration process is their participation within cultures that are characterized by a higher level of crime and violence. It is not that surprising if immigrants try their best to avoid what may be socially perceived as deviant or criminal behaviour. After all, migrants have much more to lose than so-called natives. Generally, serious criminal convictions carry with them the danger of the additional sanction of deportation and, beyond that, there is always around the migrant, as Sayad suggested (1999), a "double suspicion". "Punishment" is to the foreigner more serious than to the native and it is reasonable for migrants to be – contrary to stereotype – hyperconformists. This is even more the case once they have established themselves in their new social settings. Americans of ethnic origins felt, after a few generations, more "American" than the average member of the population. They also reached integration goals, which in terms of wealth and social prestige (Jencks 1983), were higher.

In the 1990s there was a true rediscovery of the sociological and criminological interest in the migration–crime and migration–punishment nexuses (Marshall 1997; Tonry 1997; Martinez and Valenzuela 2006; McDonald 2009; Simes and Waters 2014). This interest focused in part on the United States, and in part on a comparison between what was going on in the US and what was going on elsewhere, especially in Europe. As mentioned, the new globalization phase in worldwide socio-economic development that began in the 1980s brought an increase in migration flows that rivalled the period at the start of the twentieth century. The "liberal" revolution, kicked off under the impulse of the Thatcher and Reagan regimes in the late 1970s and early 1980s, was certainly behind such huge deployment of men and women, an event that found a phenomenal multiplier in the victory of this renewed radical variation of capitalism over the most important twentieth-century competitor, what was called at the time the "Socialist Field" or "realized Socialism". This, together with the impulse of a new economic imperialism toward many Asian, African and Latin American countries (after the failures of "third world nationalism" and the "nonaligned movement"), meant that the defeated Second and Third Worlds had to pay their tribute of men and women to the victorious First World, "the West" so called! After all, one could probably apply to migrants (labour, living capital), what David Graeber writes about debt (money, fixed capital):

> So what is the status of all this money continually being funnelled into the U.S. treasury? Are these loans? Or is it tribute? In the past, military powers that maintained hundreds of military bases outside their own home territory were ordinarily referred to as "empires", and empires regularly demanded tribute from subject peoples. The U.S. government, of course, insists that it is not an empire – but one could easily make a case that the only reason it insists on treating these payments as "loans" and not as "tribute" is precisely to deny the reality of what's going on. (Graeber 2011: 6)

Likewise, in a way not too dissimilar from when the regions annexed to the Roman Empire had to offer their quota of slaves to the Roman need for labour, starting in the 1980s, masses of Asian, African, Latin American and Eastern European peoples started to pour into the liberal-democratic field, a field that largely coincided with a "West" to be understood as a moral and political object if not a geographical one. Northern America, Europe (or the EU), Japan and other "Asian tigers" such as Hong Kong and Singapore, Australia, South Africa, Israel and the Middle East Gulf countries, became the poles of attraction of a world-wide movement of men and women.[2] However, a fundamental difference between the period in the first half of the twentieth century when migration was the main source of "Fordist" labour feeding into the assembly lines of auto makers, and the one after the 1973 oil crisis, was that no "Fordist" mass factories were going to welcome the new labour any longer. This labour would be employed instead within sectors that are certainly crucial to the functioning of the whole production machinery but marginal to the core of the process. Accordingly, the ease with which it was possible to migrate, especially in the European case, would be drastically reduced.

Migration and punishment in the United States

It is well known that the total number of people imprisoned in the United States is staggering, especially if one were to compare it with the number of prison inmates in Europe, especially Western Europe. The US imprisonment rate is above 700 per

---

[2] One should note that at least the Romans, in 212 AD, conferred Roman citizenship to the (free) inhabitants of the whole Empire! A very similar argument is developed by Juan Gonzalez about the relationship of the United States to Latin America in his *Harvest of Empire* (Gonzalez 1999).

100,000, including state and federal prison facilities plus local jails[3] (one could consider that the European average wavers around 100 per 100,000 and even those countries where there has been recently quite an increase, such as the UK, Spain and the Netherlands, are still below 150 per 100,000 [Snacken 2010: 274]). On the other hand, if one considers the *percentages* of foreigners that are part of those larger numbers, the situation reverses itself. Their number is quite contained in the United States, especially if we compare it to their numbers in Europe (as we shall see in the next chapter).

In fact, the percentage of "noncitizens" in US prisons – at least the ones counted – is officially less than the number of noncitizens in the general population. On June 30, 2010, for instance, a reported 95,977 noncitizens were held in custody of state or federal correctional authorities. Overall, about 6 per cent of state and federal inmates at midyear 2010 were not US citizens, whereas the percentage of the US population that is foreign born is about 12 per cent (an unknown proportion of which have in the meanwhile become citizens).[4] Using the foreign-born category is certainly sensible, in a country where the *ius soli* is sovereign, and, if anything, would slightly inflate the number of noncitizens, given that some who are foreign born will have acquired

---

[3]According to the Bureau for Justice Statistics (2012), on 31 December 2012, state and federal correctional authorities had jurisdiction over 1,571,013 prisoners, the third consecutive year of decline, largely due to the decrease in California state prison population (that accounted for about half of the overall decline, due to a California court decision which prescribed the reduction of overcrowding in the State, *Brown v. Plata*, a decision that was upheld in a US Supreme Court 5–4 ruling) (Simon 2014a). The 2012 imprisonment rate for the nation was 480 prisoners per 100,000 US residents (all of this does not include, however, the inmates of local jails!).

[4]We do not have data about noncitizens in county jails and is reasonable to think that their percentage in the general county jail population (perhaps because waiting for trial or punished for minor immigration law infractions) may be higher than in state prisons. Looking however at the ways in which the data about prisons are collected one wonders. According to the 2011 Bureau of Justice Statistics, in some states (Alaska, Hawaii, Massachusetts, New Jersey, South Carolina) noncitizenship is basically self-reported; in others (Colorado, Missouri, Mississippi, New York, Tennessee, Virginia) it is based on the count of foreign-born inmates (Guerino et al. 2011) or is just an "estimate" (Illinois, Kansas); in still others (Oklahoma and, crucially, California) it is based on the number of inmates held by Immigration and Customs Enforcement (ICE). Even when we consider how many foreigners are in US prisons, it is really uncertain what the sources of data are. It is safe therefore to assume that we have no way to know exactly how many noncitizens are detained in American prisons, at least in state (and county) prisons. The data that follow, collected by Rubén Rumbaut, are based on the US Census (see n. 8).

American citizenship in the meanwhile. However, all the other ways to determine the noncitizen status are likely to underestimate the number of noncitizens in a situation in which to declare one's condition of lack of citizenship may entail, especially for the more serious offenses, the risk of deportation. As we shall see, in my opinion the difficulty at determining the citizenship status is just an aspect of the American attitude toward migration and, more specifically, toward the relationship between migration and crime.

In order to explain what may, however, be perceived as counterintuitive, we have first of all to free the discussion from two possibilities about why the number of immigrants criminalized in the United States seems to be so low. The first, based on the European experience, as we shall see, is that lack of documentation and criminalization are much more closely connected, in Europe, than migrants and crime, therefore we might hypothesize that perhaps there are no foreigners in prison in the United States – or at least many fewer than in Europe, as we shall see – because in the US there are no undocumented migrants. This, however, is quite unlikely. The number of (documented) immigrants in the US has reached heights, lately, approaching the level of the 1920s. In 2010 the foreign born numbered about 40 million. At the same time, there are estimates by the Pew Research Hispanic Trends Project according to which,

> The sharp decline in the U.S. unauthorized immigrant population that accompanied the Great Recession has bottomed out, and the number may be rising again. An estimated 11.7 million unauthorized immigrants were living in the U.S. in March 2012, according to a new preliminary Pew Research Centre estimate. Different trends appear among the six states in which 60 per cent of unauthorized immigrants live – California, Florida, Illinois, New Jersey, New York and Texas. Of these, only Texas had increases in its unauthorized immigrant population between 2007 and 2011. The analysis also finds that the post-2007 population dip was sharper for Mexicans than for unauthorized immigrants as a whole. (Passel et al. 2013)

That is, both in proportion to the population and to the number of documented immigrants, numbers of undocumented migrants are much higher than in Europe today (estimated between two and three millions)![5]

There is, however, also another possibility that we have to exclude. Could it be perhaps that there are no foreigners in prison in the United States – or at least many fewer than in Europe – because they are all swiftly deported (Kanstroom 2007, 2012;

---

[5]See also Michael Hoefer, Nancy Rytina and Bryan C. Baker, *Estimates of the Unauthorized Immigrant Population Residing in the United States: January 2007*, US Department of Homeland Security, Office of Immigration Statistics, Policy Directorate, available at: www.dhs.gov/xlibrary/assets/statistics/publications/ois_ill_pe_2007.pdf; Amnesty International (2008: 4); Gonzales (2011); Passel (2006); Passel and Cohn (2010); and, most recently, Warren (2014).

King et al. 2012[6])? Each year, more than 300,000 foreigners are, in Saskia Sassen's words, "incarcerated without trial only because officialdom considered it likely that they were illegal residents" (Sassen 2010). In 2008, according to Gary E. Mead, Deputy Director of an ICE (Immigration and Customs Enforcement – Department of Homeland Security) office, "Over the last four years more than a million people have passed through ICE detention facilities. During fiscal year 2007 alone, more than 322,000 illegal aliens passed through ICE detention facilities and approximately 280,000 of those were removed from the Unites States".[7] That is, during the year, a figure that translates into an average presence of approximately 30,000 illegal aliens in ICE detention facilities every single day, and even more than that recently:

> … from 2001 to 2012, the average size of the daily noncitizen detention population increased by more than 50 per cent, from 20,429 in 2001 to 32,953 in 2012 … ICE detained 363,064 aliens during 2010. During that year, the average daily detention population was 30,885. Although more than 61 per cent of all detainees were from Mexico, they tended to have short stays in detention and, thus, they accounted for only 36 per cent of detention bed days. The other leading countries for the percentage of detention bed days were El Salvador (11 per cent), Guatemala (10 per cent), and Honduras (8 per cent). (Siskin 2012: 12)

These are big numbers, and they have been increasing dramatically in later years; however, they are in no way comparable to the incredibly larger number of inmates present in US correctional facilities. Furthermore, the drive to increase the number of deportations is quite recent, whereas the difference between first and second generation incarcerations goes back to the origins of such observations. In fact, using Census data from the year 2000 (therefore much before all of these developments) on US imprisonment divided by place of birth, Rumbaut et al. (2006: 71) showed that incarcerated foreign-born males in *all* American ethnic groups are systematically lower than incarcerated US-born males in the same groups, as appears from Table 2.1.[8]

The study by Rumbaut and his collaborators was a particularly interesting effort that came in the wake of a revival of interest, in the United States, in the nexus between migration and crime and that between migration and punishment (Hawkins 1995; Marshall 1997; Tonry 1997; Martinez and Valenzuela 2006; McDonald 2009; Bucerius and Tonry 2014). The view by sociologists of migration such as Rumbaut and others

---

[6]For a form of "domestic deportation" see Beckett and Herbert (2010).

[7]In a hearing before a Congressional Subcommittee on Immigration (13 February 2008).

[8]I thank Rubén Rumbaut for permission to reproduce this table (Rumbaut et al. 2006: 71). The data are drawn from group quarters data on institutionalized populations from the decennial census; for young men 18–39 they are overwhelmingly incarcerated populations, in state and federal prisons as well as county jails (personal communication by Rubén Rumbaut to the author).

Table 2.1   Percentage of males aged 18–39 years incarcerated in the United States, 2000, by nativity and level of education, in rank order by ethnicity

| Ethnicity (Self- reported) | Males, Ages 18–39 | | % Incarcerated, by Nativity and by Education | | | |
| | Total in US (N) | % Incarcerated | Nativity | | High School Graduate? | |
			Foreign- Born	US- Born	No	Yes
Total	45,200,417	3.04	0.86	3.51	6.91	2.00
Latin American Ethnicities						
Salvadoran, Guatemalan	433,828	0.68	0.52	3.01	0.71	0.62
Colombian, Ecuadorian, Peruvian	283,599	1.07	0.80	2.37	2.12	0.74
Mexican	5,017,431	2.71	0.70	5.90	2.84	2.55
Dominican	182,303	2.76	2.51	3.71	4.62	1.39
Cuban	213,302	3.01	2.22	4.20	5.22	2.29
Puerto Rican[a]	642,106	5.06	4.55	5.37	10.48	2.41
Asian Ethnicities						
Indian	393,621	0.22	0.11	0.99	1.20	0.14
Chinese, Taiwanese	439,086	0.28	0.18	0.65	1.35	0.14
Korean	184,238	0.38	0.26	0.93	0.93	0.34
Filipino	297,011	0.64	0.38	1.22	2.71	0.41
Vietnamese	229,735	0.89	0.46	5.60	1.88	0.55
Laotian, Cambodian	89,864	1.65	0.92	7.26	2.80	1.04
Other						
White, non-Hispanic	29,014,261	1.66	0.57	1.71	4.64	1.20
Black, non-Hispanic	5,453,546	10.87	2.47	11.61	21.33	7.09
Two or more race groups, other	1,272,742	3.09	0.72	3.85	6.24	2.24

Source: 2000 US Census, 5% PUMS. Data are estimates for adult males, ages 18 to 39, in correctional institutions at the time of the census.

[a] Island-born Puerto Ricans, who are US citizens by birth and not immigrants, are classified as "foreign born" for purposes of this table; mainland-born Puerto Ricans are here classified under "US born".

Table reproduced with permission from New York University Press. Source: Rumbaut, Rubén G., Roberto G. Gonzales, Golnaz Komaie, Charlie V. Morgan and Rosaura Tafoya-Estrada (2006) 'Immigration and Incarceration: Patterns and Predictors of Imprisonment among First- and Second-Generation Young Adults', in R. Martinez Jr and A. Valenzuela (eds), *Immigration and Crime: Race, Ethnicity and Violence.* New York: New York University Press, p. 71.

like him is strictly linked with the concept of *labour market segmentation*. Contrary to neoclassical economic theory, according to which the labour market is a perfect market where everybody is competing with everybody else and the worst jobs will then go to those who have the least skills and the higher propensities to hard or dangerous work, the idea of *market segmentation* is instead the idea that there are invisible markers based in history, tradition and culture that make certain jobs more readily available to certain people, even if they are not necessarily, in abstract, those fittest for the job. Ascriptive social characteristics, such as perceptions of class, gender, race and status, become therefore some of the determinant forces in the structuration of the job market. Rumbaut owed to the perspective of leading migration scholars, like Alejandro Portes (Rumbaut and Portes 2001), the view that second generation children would follow a path of downward mobility into a sort of "underclass" where they would join a section of the native-born – a kind of "downward assimilation". They find themselves within urban environments haunted by labour market segmentation, class barriers and racial discrimination. It is what Rumbaut and Ewing (2007) have called "the paradox of assimilation" (Berardi and Bucerius 2014: 554).

Contrary to the destiny of first generations, these groups of native-born youths would find themselves in danger of joining within excluded and marginalized sections of American society in the same hopeless and negative social destiny. The results of Rumbaut's analysis on the connection between first generations, second generations and risk of imprisonment, seem to give credence to such predictions. On the contrary, children of immigrants resembling the most fortunate sections of American society would be less at risk of such outcome. Rumbaut was therefore able to mobilize the traditional explanation of the Chicago School about so-called ethnic niches in order to explain the very low imprisonment rate of first generations.[9] Furthermore, he draws attention to the fact that the various ethnic groups have very different incarceration rates from each other but, within each group, US-born have higher rates than foreign-born within the same group. Rumbaut explains that, in the shift from first to second generation, not only does one exit the somewhat conservative and protective warmth of one's ethnic niche but also at the same time enters a wider world that is characterized – as the old Chicago School vulgate would go – by heterogeneity, mobility and anonymity, thereby crucially lowering "natural" social controls. In sum, a number of recent studies have come to the conclusion that if crime and migration are in any way related, they are because actually "immigration reduces crime", a position that has been characterized as an "emerging scholarly consensus" in the United States (Hagan and Palloni 1999; Butcher and Piehl 2007; Hagan et al. 2008; Sampson 2008; Lee and Martinez 2009; Ousey and Kubrin 2009; Davies and Fagan 2012: 105; Simes and Waters 2014).

---

[9]With the proviso, of course, that imprisonment cannot be taken in any way as a proxy for crime and that there are reasons to think that first generations' imprisonment may be quite underestimated due to the ways in which noncitizenship is counted in state penal statistics.

Sociology of migration and criminology: labelling theory

Another important connection may be established between sociology of migration and sociology of deviance, and this turns on the centrality of the concept of "stigma" in the sociology of deviance (Goffman 1963). The work by Cecilia Menjívar and Leisy J. Abrego (2012: 1382–5) is particularly important here. They write of what they call "legal violence".[10] One of the effects of legal violence is to transform migrants into "outlaws" in face of the "stigma" that is inscribed onto them (Menjívar and Abrego 2012: 1409). There is also, at the same time, a logic of "racialization" at work, i.e. the construction of an inferior "other" – as Calavita comments on the Southern European case (Calavita 2005: 144–56). As we have seen, the sociology of migration tells us how "second generation" children face the prospect of a "downward assimilation" within a labour market that is "segmented" according to class, gender and national origins (Piore 1979). Their integration is basically a subordinate form of integration, and they would therefore also share in a reality of street crime that is strictly connected to the whole phenomenon of downward assimilation.

In another paper, but commenting on the same data, Rumbaut notices that "the data ... suggest ... a story of segmented assimilation to the criminal propensities of the native-born" (Rumbaut 2008: 11). The term "criminal propensities" – as in Marx's sentence quoted at the beginning of this work (see p. 6) – is always more than a bit ambiguous because it is unclear whether it refers to some kind of higher statistical likelihood (the source of which remains obscure) or to some kind of "innate" criminal predisposition. This is where it seems to me that the contribution of the sociology of deviance becomes crucial – especially some of the findings, typical of 1960s and 1970s sociology, that at the time went under the heading of "labelling", a labelling "theory" or "approach". Both sociologists of migration and traditional criminologists seem to have – for quite different reasons – underestimated the importance of labelling, a labelling that is not only the result of the (generally) low socio-economic status of migrants and of the neighbourhoods where they live (Sampson 2012), but also of the legal status that migrants hold (even if, as we shall see, in Europe and in America the labelling effect seems to function in a different manner).

The fact of the matter is that the issue of labelling, especially in Edwin M. Lemert's version of "secondary deviation" (1951), is strictly linked to what Rumbaut calls

---

[10]It seems to me that the concept of "legal violence" or the traditional idea of "criminalization" from the sociology of deviance are more adequate concepts for describing what is going on here than the recent emphasis on "crimmigration" (Stumpf 2006), a concept that, even if formulated with critical intentions, may end up reinforcing the idea of a necessary connection between "crime" and "migration" instead of criticizing it (see also Kaufman 2013).

"downward assimilation". It may well be seen as the social-psychological representation of its more structural dimension. A (downward) "segmented assimilation framework" not only means in fact a somewhat forced insertion into the lowest rungs of a "segmented labour market" but, even before that, means assimilation within the poorest sections of the city, characterized by relative deprivation and very often policed, especially in the urban areas of the United States, very aggressively. As Edwin Sutherland wrote, as a young criminology professor, in the first edition of his future epoch-making *Criminology*:

> Poverty in the modern city generally means segregation in low-rent sections, where people are isolated from many of the cultural influences and forced into contact with many of the degrading influences. Poverty generally means a low status, with little to lose, little to respect, little to be proud of, little to sustain efforts to improve. It generally means bad housing conditions, lack of sanitation in the vicinity, and lack of attractive community institutions. It generally means both parents being away from home for long hours, with the fatigue, lack of control of children, and irritation that go with these. It generally means withdrawal of the child from school at an early age and the beginning of mechanical labour, with weakening of the home control, the development of anti-social grudges, and lack of cultural contacts. Poverty, together with the display of wealth in shop-windows, streets, and picture shows, generally means envy and hatred of the rich and the feeling of missing much in life, because of the lack of satisfaction of the fundamental wishes. Poverty seldom forces people to steal or become prostitutes in order to escape starvation. It produces its effects most frequently on the attitudes, rather than on the organism. But it is surprising how many poor people are not made delinquents, rather than how many are made delinquents. (Sutherland 1924: 169–70)[11]

A connection becomes established then between a poor self-image – who would be proud of living in such areas? – and an active role of the police and welfare agencies in general in emphasizing that self-image is after all quite right! Why, however, would this not happen to first generations? A crucial distinction between first and second generations lies in the social processes that have brought them to the American soil and that have governed their upbringing. The first generation immigrant is often a noncitizen, responsible for his new condition, happy to have found work and to make a living, who thinks of "success", in the traditional American way, as only a possibility, to which however he or she is not "entitled" in the common sense in which a "real American" would feel entitled to it! The latter is instead – as we have already seen discussing the Chicago School – the perspective of his or her children, who find themselves in America exactly in the same way in which other American children find themselves there, without ever having "chosen" to be there, and with the same expectations, as

---

[11]I owe my attention to this passage to Wayne Morrison's *Theoretical Criminology* (1995: 248).

to equality of entitlement and destiny, as any other American child. The experience of downward assimilation is to them therefore particularly frustrating and unpleasant, for some of the reasons that, as we have seen, were first advanced by Merton.

Unfortunately, however, the precious insights of the labelling approach are by and large no longer available to American sociologists and criminologists, at least in their "mainstream" component. The 1970s revanchism in criminology, when the labelling approach was (rightly) perceived as belonging in the 1960s rebellious mood and was swept away by cultural changes linked to the Reagan and Thatcher conservative reaction, made the wisdom of that scepticism substantially unavailable to the social sciences that followed (Rock 2005). This was a pity, because the resistance of sociologists of migration against the onslaught of nativist reaction would have greatly benefited from reflecting on the perverse results of racism and xenophobia toward the production of crime and, at the same time, of penal repression, among the most marginal sectors of the American and British lower classes, among which were the migrants.[12]

A special and, in the United States, crucial, aspect of this story is what concerned African American (domestic) immigration from the South. We have seen how, after the introduction in 1924 of a "quota" system to contain "undesirable" alien populations, the mass migration of African American rural workers from the South to the North developed enormously (Wilkerson 2010). Jonathan Simon (2014b) has noted, in a recent reconstruction of the roots of radical criminology in the United States, that the precondition of what would then later happen, especially in the centres of the new American society, such as California, was the labour situation created by World War II, when millions of white males, the core of the industrial workforce, were drafted into or volunteered for the army. However, workers were still badly needed in order to produce what was necessary in order to wage war against Germany and Japan. The areas of potential new labour to which industry then turned were women and blacks. As a consequence, thousands of blacks and whites from the rural South moved to the Bay Area and LA, as well as to other industrial core areas of the country, in order to join the new workforce. Exclusion and isolation by race – Simon adds – began in this era and so did reliance on the police to enforce it. Furthermore, once the war was over, a massive drop in industrial jobs followed. With veterans coming home, women and blacks were pushed out of the workforce.

The second generation to those African Americans who had migrated were the protagonists of 1960s and 1970s struggles. People such as Huey Newton and Bobby Seale, who were to become the founders of the Black Panthers Party in the Bay Area, were children and nephews to those who had moved westward (Simon 2014). And,

---

[12] However, in the recent ethnographies by such authors as Victor Rios (2011) and Alice Goffman (2014) a labelling perspective seems to re-emerge and come back with a vengeance.

although police violence in the Bay Area had been a constant for blacks, there is reason to believe that, in the 1960s, this violence intensified in response to the efforts of black youth to act on the opportunities that the new economy and new civil rights laws were supposed to protect. Thereafter, the Panthers became subject to the most determined effort by the federal government, especially the FBI, to destroy a domestic political movement, whereas the young black and brown men and women they sought to organize, as well as – and even more – their children and nephews and nieces, became, after the defeat, the major victims of mass incarceration.[13]

The paradox of migration

The new immigration act of 1965 changed the situation again, abolishing the quota and thereby setting limits no longer to Southern Europeans but to Latin Americans (Simes and Waters 2014: 467–9). However, the following reforms of 1986 and 1996 introduced further restrictions, in a political climate in which anti-immigrant sentiment again became vociferous (Campesi 2013: 114–19). An important aspect of the 1996 reform was section 287(g), according to which the federal government was allowed to set up agreements with state and local law enforcement agencies, allowing them to perform immigration law enforcement functions. When, after September 11, 2001, the so-called "Patriot Act"[14] and especially the "Homeland Security Act",[15] introduced further repressive measures (Kanstroom 2007, 2012) and created the new and rather menacingly called ICE (Immigration and Customs Enforcement), the overall resulting tendency was one of "criminalizing" "immigration law". Whereas deportation increased quite a bit, the number of foreigners in jail – i.e., seriously criminalized – in the United States remained quite low, especially if compared to Europe, as we shall see. In understanding this fact, in my view, a very important aspect is legal status and consideration of the efforts of the various branches of law enforcement to ascertain such status. I would claim that legal citizenship status, even if certainly of growing importance in many American state legislatures, is incomparably less important in

---

[13]On this transition, cf. the documentary film "Bastards of the Party", directed by Cle Sloan (USA, 2006) and see Brotherton (2008a, 2008b), Venkatesh (2008), Rios (2011) and Goffman (2014).

[14]A legislative measure passed into law under President George W. Bush shortly after the attacks on the Twin Towers and other American targets, which enhanced "security" and gave broad powers to the federal government in many aspects of American life.

[15]Passed in 2002 created the Department of Homeland Security, which acquired new powers also on matters of immigration.

the United States than within member states of the European Union. I would also claim that even less meaningful and (especially) less pervasive are the efforts in the US to ascertain such status. In other words, one possible explanation of the lower relationship between migration, even undocumented migration, and processes of criminalization in the US is the relative ease with which, in the US, it is possible to "pass" as citizens or anyway regular, documented aliens. Paramount in this is the position of local police departments, which in spite of the recent efforts by federal agencies and a few states, generally are quite uninterested in the citizenship status of the people they encounter except if in connection with a crime committed (even if, as we shall see, recent federal and state legislation tried to change exactly this aspect, until, at least, Obama's speech and executive actions on migration of November 20, 2014, which seemed to backtrack on that orientation). The very difficulty of even knowing how many noncitizens are actually detained in state prisons – that we have seen above – is, after all, part of this general attitude.

This would indeed seem like a true paradox of migration. In the United States it may be easier (than in Europe) for a foreign citizen to integrate him- or herself because of the *lack* of a national identity document and of the attendant policies, which may facilitate hiring based on the false assumption of citizenship, and therefore increase the likelihood of employment and "making an honest living". The greater ease with which undocumented migrants may deceive potential employers, as well as authorities, in the United States,[16] might protect them – and American society! – from the risk of (other kinds of) crime,[17] whereas the European obsession with discovering migrant crime may increase the likelihood of its occurrence. This possibility is intensified by the fact that, in many European countries, it is the business of ordinary police forces to control and check on strangers. As yet, this is something that is not as pervasive in

---

[16]Is this myth or reality about the American immigration experience? Even if it were only myth, however, we know that myths have a deep influence on the ways in which people – last but not least control officers – perceive their role in society. It brings to mind that wonderful film by Elia Kazan, *America America* (see the image on the front cover), where the protagonist, after having committed some horrendous crimes in a heroic effort to travel from his original Anatolia (in Turkey) to the America he had so much longed for, finally on Ellis Island is christened a new man with a new name, Joe Arness! Or, outside of fiction and more recently, the self-disclosure of an award-winning Filipino journalist, José Antonio Vargas, who publicly revealed his irregular immigration status – which had lasted almost his lifetime – and the vicissitudes that made a successful life possible even under such circumstances (Vargas 2011).

[17]Whereas, "as Massey, Durand, and Malone (2002) have noted, the [recent] stiffer immigration restrictions may have the unintended consequences of increasing the number of undocumented immigrants" (Kil and Menjívar 2006: 167–8) and therefore, I would add, of crime.

the US, although this is precisely what legislation passed in Arizona and other states would encourage (something, however, that did not go uncontested if it is true that, in May 2010, the City Council of Los Angeles decided to boycott the state of Arizona because of its immigration bill – given that in this city the police behaviour called for in the Arizona law[18] would indeed be highly problematic!).[19]

Undocumented migrants who "pass" as documented are able to find regular jobs or anyway to make a living, without resorting to crime (except perhaps crimes committed to the purpose of "passing", such as, for instance, forgeries) therefore protecting themselves, and the possible victims, from the attaining risks. The drive within America at the time of writing, in many states, such as Arizona, Alabama, South Carolina, Georgia, Utah and Indiana, to introduce a number of hardships and restrictions on "illegal" immigration would go in the direction of putting much more pressure onto undocumented migrants and introducing greater coordination between federal agencies such as ICE and local police forces. Such pressure would probably have the perverse effect of adding to the criminalization and brutalization that are already typical of the US–Mexico border, making the United States increasingly similar to the EU (Kil and Menjívar 2006; Kil et al. 2009; Beckett and Herbert 2010). Cecilia Menjívar, with Sang H. Kil and Roxanne L. Doty (2009), and later with Leisy J. Abrego (2012), has done extensive ethnographic work with immigrants in the American South-West and has come to the conclusion that this conjunction of criminalization processes and immigration law breeds what first William Bowers and Glenn Pierce (1980), then Dane Archer and Rosemary Gartner (1984) called "brutalization", noting in fact that harsh, violent and unlawful governmental action breeds a "legitimation of violence" (Melossi 2008: 165), which is a further aspect of "legal violence". A vicious circle would therefore become established between crime, especially violent crime, and punitive social reaction, especially severely punitive social reaction. Archer and Gartner cite what Justice Louis Brandeis stated in 1928: "Our government is the potent, the omnipresent teacher. For good or ill, it teaches

---

[18]Which would allow among other things the possibility for ordinary local police to enquire about the citizenship status of people stopped, an aspect of the Arizona law the constitutionality of which was affirmed by the US Supreme Court on 25 June 2012 (other aspects of the law were instead struck down).

[19]In a related development, at the beginning of 2013 Oakland became the first city to offer municipal identity cards to undocumented migrants that also work as debit cards. Municipal ID cards were already issued in New Haven, Connecticut and San Francisco. More recently, after Bill De Blasio became Mayor of New York, New York too adopted a similar resolution. According to city officials, these cards encourage undocumented immigrants to interact with police without fear of deportation, and increase the likelihood of reporting about labour and housing violations.

the whole people by its example. Crime is contagious. If the government becomes a lawbreaker, it breeds contempt for the law" (cited in Archer and Gartner 1984: 95).

A minor paradoxical aspect within this more general situation is that one of the consequences of the introduction of norms such as section 287(g) is that,

> harsh legal sanctions against immigrants are often framed as a means to keep communities "safe", yet they may in fact have the opposite effect by decreasing cooperation with police. In fact recent studies show that cynicism of the police and the legal system not only leads to an increased likelihood of neighbourhood crime and violence but also undermines individuals' willingness to cooperate with the police and to engage in the collective actions necessary to socially control crime. (Kirk et al. 2011: 4–5)

In other words, the introduction of harsher and more restrictive norms and provisions on "illegal" immigration, contrary to the stated goal of protecting the American citizenry, would probably have the perverse effect of adding to the criminalization and brutalization of undocumented migrants, increasingly unable to "pass" as documented and therefore to find regular jobs (or anyway, to make a living), without resorting to crime. Thus, this would make the United States increasingly similar to Europe in the processes of criminalization of immigration and also of crimes committed by migrants – a true textbook case of the *labelling* process, by which the very operation of the law, by persecuting deviance, breeds and feeds ever-new forms of the same.

Were that not enough, however, such overall changes in immigration law and enforcement would also represent a profound betrayal of a specific "American" tradition, because such greater ease with "passing" and even "lying" is after all related to a greater American tolerance for innovation and the idea of "getting another chance", the idea, that is, that one can reinvent oneself – like Joe Arness! – and that, if given a chance, he or she may become a different person, free of the shackles of tradition, parentage, language, faith or custom. The American celebration of the outlaw is, after all, a celebration of being, literally, outside of the law. This is an attitude that is also somehow connected with the deeply ingrained American tradition of *ius soli*, the principle according to which the acquisition of citizenship is grounded in being born within the territory of the United States. This is typical of an immigrant nation: it welcomes those who arrive to the new soil and tries to strengthen the link of the newcomers to their newly found land. Quite contrary is the policy of e-migrant countries, which go by the principle instead of *ius sanguinis*, or the law of the blood, in trying to hold on to the descendants of its emigrants, as has been the case of Italy, for instance.[20]

---

[20]In the United States, the principle of *ius soli* was recognized in the Fourteenth Amendment to the US Constitution (1868) and was then restated in a 1898 Supreme Court ruling (*US* v. *Wong Kim Ark*) that declared that a child born to noncitizens (even if ineligible for naturalization), on American soil, is, in fact, an American citizen.

This favour traditionally accorded to migrants has another side to the coin, however. This shows up in the transition from the criminalization of the first generation to the criminalization of successive generations, as we have seen from Rumbaut's studies. Whereas, in each ethnic group, we see an increase of committals to prison for the citizen generations *vis à vis* the noncitizens, there is, however, a deep difference between group and group. More specifically, blacks, Latinos and Indo-Chinese fare much worse than white and "traditional" Asian groups. In other words, the question of immigration seems to convert almost immediately, in the United States, into an issue of "race" and ethnic minority. It is not immigrants as such who are feared, despised and emarginated, but specific groups defined on the basis of their *"race"*, however conceived and constructed (Takaki 1979; Gilroy 1987; Davis 1990). Of course, as Park and others pointed out, immigrant groups have their histories, and the most stigmatized may in time attain respectability. This was the case for European groups, such as Irish, Jewish and Italian people. Or the Chinese and Japanese among the Asian groups. And so, the profile of "danger" has always been attached, in the United States, to a racial profile, rather than a national one. The case of the Italian group is particularly interesting. Attentive to statements such as the one by Lombroso mentioned at the opening of this present work, and more generally to the anthropological theories of the time, American immigration authorities at the start of the twentieth century used to distinguish carefully between Northern Italians, to be considered as white, and Southern Italians, whose racial prerogatives were uncertain and who should be treated with much more caution. Here too the degree of criminalization of migrants is a function of the attitudes towards them, and a sensitivity to the issue of "labelling" is therefore a key element in a more serviceable account of migration phenomena.

The rhetoric of the "nation of immigrants" is definitely present in President Obama's speech of 20 November 2014, announcing comprehensive immigration reform. Such rhetoric may be related to the fact that punishment of immigrants is distinctively low in the United States, both compared to punishment of second generations, as we have seen, and also compared to punishment of immigrants in Europe and generally in countries which do not describe themselves as "immigration countries". Of course this is a function also of immigrants' participation in behaviour that can easily be criminalized. Here the tradition of sociology of deviance and especially what in the 1960s was called "labelling" may become particularly useful because it sheds light on the fact that people, and therefore also immigrants, tend to adapt themselves to the roles, personalities and characteristics that are predicated about them: in other words, that we tend to become the kind of people we are said to be.

THREE

crime, punishment and migration in an age of globalization: Europe

We have seen that, in the case of the United States, the hostility toward an immigrant "other", even if certainly present at different times in the history of the country, almost always yielded, especially in the perspective of elites, to the rhetoric of the immigrant country. A see-saw of hatred and love for the stranger has accompanied the various stages in the social and economic development of the United States. At times the stranger was celebrated as part of a cosmopolitan urban wealth in periods of prosperity and progress, at other times execrated as a sacrificial scapegoat, in periods of crisis, depression and misery. The stranger's destiny in Europe, however, has been quite different. Here, the rhetoric of the country of immigration – perhaps with the partial exception of France and the UK – has been sorely lacking. On the contrary, Europe has been, in most cases, a constellation of statelets that have routinely hoped to solve their economic, social and political problems by sending away a good part of their younger generation, usually the strongest and liveliest of them, those for whom it was hardest to endure the "holy" alliance of reactionary gentry "aristocracy", conservative church leaders and industrial lords that has weighed so heavily for such a long time, and with such nefarious consequences, over the history of Europe (Gramsci 1929–1935).

Crime, punishment and migration in Europe

In the nineteenth and early twentieth centuries, most European countries were emigrant countries, especially toward the Americas and later on also to Australia. There is sometimes the idea that migration should be linked to some kind of "poverty".

However, migratory movements usually take place when at least a certain threshold of "modernization" has been reached (Castles and Miller 2009). This is for a number of reasons. First, mere "subsistence" economies do not really produce the "excess" population that finds its way into emigration. It is typical instead of agricultural economies on their way to development that an increase in the productivity of agriculture should bring about an increase in the rural population but without the possibility of their finding suitable employment in the local economy. Furthermore, the country of emigration has to be enough integrated within a "world system" to make migrations practically possible, logistically and otherwise. Especially, it has to be enough part of a world-wide culture to allow the members of its "excess" population to think that a move might be positive, and to hold some kind of, however confused, representation of such possibility, not to mention the personal ambition to be part of it. Migratory movements are in this sense much more a product of development than of poverty, or better, we may think of it as poverty *within* development.

So, various European countries in turn, when they had reached a certain level of development, experienced emigration, a movement that, as we mentioned at the beginning, largely concerns a transformation of peasants into industrial workers, or in any case *urban* workers. For instance, English and Scottish people left Great Britain in the eighteenth and early nineteenth centuries; Irish people and Germans left their countries in the second half of the nineteenth century, when also French and Northern Italian people started migrating to the United States, Brazil and Argentina. Later on, the great European migration between 1880 and World War I concerned Southern and Eastern Europeans. We have seen that this last European migration was linked to a period of extensive industrial production of durable goods for mass consumption, first in the United States but then, also, thanks to the American hegemony that followed World War II, throughout the Western world. We have seen also how this "Fordist" style of mass production was especially geared toward hiring a recent working class without industrial skills, a mass of former peasants who, by moving toward the centres of industrial development, could easily be employed and find a job. This happened also in Europe, after World War II, thanks to the funds of the Marshall Plan and the following economic reconstruction. The so-called "economic miracle" put to work an increasing number of former European peasants, first from the local countryside of industrial areas, then increasingly from Southern Europe.

In 1997, a very interesting book edited by Michael Tonry was published, which attempted to analyse, case by case, the situation of *Ethnicity, Crime, and Immigration* (1997) in a number of countries, mostly European.[1] So, for instance, Hans-Jörg

---

[1]This should be compared with the recent one edited by Sandra M. Bucerius and the same Michael Tonry (2014).

Albrecht, commenting on the situation in Germany at the time, pointed out that, in the transition from the Fordist period to post-Fordism, the place of origin of the immigrants changed, from within the European Union to outside the EU. Furthermore, Albrecht mentioned that another crucial change that accompanied such transition was social "segmentation" "along ethnic lines" of the kind we have already seen for the United States (Albrecht 1997: 37). In other words, the type of incorporation into production and into society that was typical of the Fordist factory was predicated on what we could call a subordinate but equal assimilation. In that context, the democracy of the assembly line prevailed. Treating all workers like subhuman components of a giant machine, such "democracy" guaranteed their equality, with no consideration of nationality, gender or "race/ethnicity".[2] This had not been the least relevant aspect of the increasing strength of a unionized working class between the 1930s and the 1960s, and it would be an important aspect also in understanding the backlash against that strength that started in the 1970s. Such a backlash would centre both around the path of alternative modes of production – especially the new information technology (as a product and as means for production) – and that of exploiting new sources from which to draw a softer and more docile working class, such as migration. The latter was in fact increasingly segmented between a small, upper- and highly skilled level, and a mass of lower-end workers no longer crucial to the production core (such as in construction, maintenance, repair and cleaning services, food and entertainment industries, not to mention the increasing section of marginal or illegal work, such as the illegal drug industry and sex work). Such segmentation was at the same time deeply connected to a process of rising inequalities everywhere in the Western world – an inequality that was in turn tightly related to rising processes of criminalization and penality (Western 2006).

This overall process was part of the "globalization" of all social issues and practices that took place between the 1990s and the crisis that started in 2007–8 (Aas 2007). On the one hand, this may have introduced an increasing "cosmopolitanism" and there are indeed authors who emphasized such a possibility (Gilroy 1993; Beck 1997; Hudson 2008). On the other hand, a fundamental contradiction was increasingly revealed, between the incessant development of processes of globalization started in the 1970s and the fact that migration control was still, after all, entrusted to nation states (Sassen 1991). Slowly, in the course of the twentieth century, and at very different times, practically all the Western and Southern European countries stopped being mainly e-migration countries and became mainly im-migration countries. This issue acquired a specific "constitutional" flavour in the case of the European Union,

---

[2]Once of course they were admitted into the factory which, for many minorities for instance, was certainly not to be taken for granted.

where the question of migration, and particularly of migration control, essentially remained a prerogative of the old nineteenth-century state power in spite of the fact that, within the latest wave of EU treaties, the whole area of "freedom, security and justice", of which migration is part, was being "communitarized". With the rise of the EU, in fact, moving from a European state to another can no longer be called "migration", at least of an external nature, because with the Schengen agreements (1985–90), a principle of free movement of persons within the area of the treaty (which overlaps only in part with the membership of the EU) became established. Between the treaties of Maastricht (1993) and Lisbon (2009), the conditions of being a "foreigner" and a "migrant" started being reserved therefore to citizens of countries outside the EU and the whole issue of migration became progressively "harmonized", even if the substance of decisions about residency and citizenship are still in the hands of the member states (with European citizenship being essentially an extension of national citizenship plus a few, minor, additional powers[3]). The fragmentation of the norms on residency and citizenship among the various European states makes the comparison between the various countries quite difficult on this terrain, and even more difficult is the valuation of the criminal aspects of migration, because an additional fragmentation is introduced by criminal norms that vary wildly from state to state (without even mentioning the variability in their enforcement).

Kitty Calavita has cogently shown the nexus between the paradoxes of current migration, especially in Southern Europe, and the requirements of a "post-Fordist" economy (Castells 1996; De Giorgi 2002; Calavita 2005; Lacey 2008; Lee 2011), i.e. an economy characterized by deindustrialization and the replacement of traditional industrial work (stable, unionized, tendentially local and male, within the core of the overall economic system) by a more "marginal" kind of employment (service sector, non-unionized, employing migrants, women and young people). A dualistic (at the very least) economy, therefore, where unskilled labour is relegated to the margins of the productive process, whereas at the same time, there is a true "explosion" (at least in good economic times) of "immaterial" work in the information economy, in financial sectors and generally in self-employed work. There is also a bifurcation in the "moral economy" of the working class (Thompson 1971) between a respectable "old" working class (on its way out), expressing moral indignation at the mores of the newcomers, and a "new", entering working class, subject of extensive processes of criminalization.

---

[3]At the time of the discussion on the Maastricht Treaty, Italian Europarliamentarian Renzo Imbeni (PDS) asked to frankly recognize a concept of European citizenship independent from individual national citizenships (Imbeni 1993), a citizenship therefore that could have been extended to individuals from non-member states. In the end the proposal was so distorted in discussion that Imbeni himself decided to vote against it and citizenship was attributed only to citizens of the member nation-states.

This whole social process is the phenomenon I have elsewhere called the "cycle of production (and re-production) of *la canaille*" (the rabble), the process, that is, by which the urban working class is cyclically replenished through the absorption of former rural strata, often through migratory movements, and the temporary creation of an urban "underclass". Thereafter usually follows the "elevation" of the former *"canaille"* – through class struggle, conflict and demands for formal rights recognition – into a proper "working class" (Melossi 2008: 229–52), even if, at each new (long) economic cycle, what is "working class" may correspond to a new and completely different reality.

In the "globalization" era that started between the 1980s and 1990s – also as a result of what it seemed at the time to be the accomplished status of the United States as the only super-power left – the conditions of immigration in each specific country were still the result of the encounter of large-scale migratory movement on a global scale with governments' attempts at somehow *regulating* immigration, or more often at *controlling* immigration (van der Leun 2003; Calavita 2005). One of the peculiar results of this encounter, which was often a mismatch, has been the extensive presence of so-called "irregular" or "undocumented" migrants, i.e. people who, according to the norms of the country where they find themselves (norms that are often very far from clear, not to mention the modalities of their enforcement), are wanting in some aspects or other in order to be considered as legally present in the territory. Van der Leun has pointed out that the situation is further complicated by the fact that the types of illegality may pertain to at least three different dimensions: entry, residence and employment (van der Leun 2003: 18–20). In any case, today estimates of undocumented migrants hover around 11–12 millions in the United States and "only" 2–3 millions in the EU!

This constitutes the sociological background to the fact that, in Europe, "the number of [foreign] suspects and convicts is considerably higher than the proportion of the foreign population" (Killias 2011: 2). Joanne van der Leun (2003) has emphasized the importance of "illegal" or "undocumented" immigrants with reference to the Dutch context but it seems to me that such emphasis may be extended also to many other "national" situations. Both immigrants in Southern Europe and asylum seekers in Central and Northern Europe have had to rely on illegal entry (or stay) methods in order to enter EU territory (Oxfam 2005: 35, Morrison 2000: 26, both cited in Lee 2011: 57). In a way that is relevant also to other European countries, such as Germany (Albrecht 1997), van der Leun highlights various stages in the management of immigration in several European countries. So, for instance, at the height of "Fordist" development in the 1950s and 1960s European "economic miracle" – tightly connected with the post-war reconstruction and the funds of the Marshall Plan – there was a "need" for a mass of unskilled labourers who could go and replenish the positions in the assembly lines of car factories and other durable goods industries. This would enable them to acquire a work permit and subsequently a residence permit. As van der Leun astutely notices, "[t]he initiative of the immigrants was seen [back then] as a sign of motivation rather than an unlawful act, and their 'illegal' status was often only a matter of time" (2003: 16–17). One could note, criminologically speaking, that in this period, migrants who would come to the Netherlands looking for work were seen as Mertonian "legal" innovators! In fact, other criminological research in that period also came to the conclusion that, in spite of a similar initial "moral panic" about migrants and their crimes, their contribution to criminal activity was often inferior to the natives' contribution (Ferracuti 1968; Kaiser 1974; Albrecht 1997). The situation was soon to change, however, with the "oil crisis" of 1973 – representing the "great divide" between the Fordist and post-Fordist periods – and the increasing deindustrialization of many European (and non-European) countries, even if in the Netherlands, for instance, the 1980s were still "years of tolerance" and it was only in the 1990s that they caught up with the general inversion of trend, and a tougher stance on "illegal" immigration and asylum came to the fore (van der Leun 2003: 17).

Italy, and Southern Europe generally, seems to me to have followed a similar path, probably with the main difference being the peculiar irrationality of immigration laws that would appear to have had a distinct "criminogenic" effect. Here too the familiar complaint was raised that "our data undoubtedly show that foreigners in our country commit a disproportionate amount of crimes relative to their number" (Barbagli 2008: 104), even if this statement is immediately qualified by the circumstance that the authors of these crimes are for the great majority *undocumented* foreigners. Crocitti reports data by which the percentages of "illegal" immigrants among the total of migrants charged with crime varies between 60 and 80 per cent according to the type of crime (Crocitti 2014: 816–18). The Caritas (2009) organization has shown that, in Italy, foreigners' contribution to crime rates – measured by reports to the police – is very close to the rate for Italians, especially if one takes into consideration the demographic profile of the two groups.[4] Crocitti (2014) shows the heavy emphasis that has been placed in Italy on issues of "emergency" and "public security" rather than on rational planning of reception, producing distorted "criminogenic" effects (in other words, illegality). Valeria Ferraris (2009) has shown how Italian immigration law forces foreigners to search for legal status through illegality. Because the annual entry quota has been transformed *de facto* into an amnesty for people already in Italy, due to

---

[4]Also in Germany, at least until the 1990s, the disproportionality in foreigners' participation in criminal activities as measured through police data is strongly reduced once the non-residential population is excluded and the demographic differences between Germans and foreigners are accounted for (Albrecht 1997: 59, 87).

an unrealistic system of matching supply and demand for labour, Italian immigration law produces "institutionalized irregularity". Foreigners enter illegally, find a job in the underground economy and then try to "fix the papers" once in Italy. They use illegality – to the point of committing crimes – in order to become legal. Migrants implement strategies to overcome their precarious condition. True Mertonian innovators, they understand that the achievement of legal status is attractive because at least it means being safe from deportation. The success of the adopted strategies largely depends on the ability of migrants to understand the essential features of the host country and to exploit the available opportunities. Looking for a way to legality – Ferraris concludes (2009) – they reveal the essential features of the Italian way of life. Furthermore, in the research work of Giuseppe Campesi on detention centres (Campesi 2015) and Giulia Fabini on the interaction between migrants and the police (Fabini forthcoming), a common element emerging is the emphasis on the modalities of (illegal) inclusion and incorporation much more than those of exclusion, as it would appear in much "criminology of mobility". Campesi points at the "undeportability" of migrants and their resistance within detention centres. Giulia Fabini looks at the ways in which the permanence on Italian soil is the outcome of a complex interaction among police officers, courts and migrants in which migrants are by no means passive subjects!

In connection with all this, it seems to me very important to emphasize that police and criminal justice statistics about foreigners are the product of what we might want to call the *double dark number of foreign crime*. Not only are the crimes reported to the police an unknown percentage out of a much larger universe of committed crimes, as is usually the case (in fact sociologists and criminologists refer to that larger universe of crime as the "dark number of crime"). If we take surfacing crime as an indicator of the (greater) submerged area of all the crimes committed, the problem is that the process of (social) selection from one to the other tends to focus on street crimes (as opposed to middle-class crimes), therefore it is a selection inherently unfavourable to migrants. All of this is well known to criminologists. My point is, however, that, on top of that, the crimes for which we are able to have a "known suspect" are in turn only a percentage of all the known crimes, many of which do not have a suspect (one has only to think of many forms of theft, crimes that, even if reported, hardly ever get to the formulation of an actual indictment). A known suspect is, however, clearly essential in order to determine a (possibly) foreign identity. For instance, in the Italian case, an estimate of the crimes for which there is at least an indictment – let alone a conviction! – out of the universe of all possible crimes committed, is slightly less than one in ten (Melossi 2010b: 454; Crocitti 2014: 810–11). Consider further that many of the crimes in which a suspect is identified are crimes that are the product of police investigation, and not of citizens' reports to the police: drug-related crimes for instance. The social procedures according to which the crimes where there is a suspect are selected out of the universe of all the crimes known – which is itself already the product of a selection process – constitute the phenomena that lead me to speak of a *"double dark number of foreign crime"*. Isn't there in fact a bias, in such double selection, against migrants, specific ethnic groups, and poor and marginal people? The bias is never against the same group everywhere, but it would represent a denial of the whole history of sociology and criminology were one to say that such bias is non-existent. We should rather say that what is usually found to be scarcely existent is evidence of direct, subjective, *intentional* discrimination against migrants or minorities (Killias 2011; Solivetti 2010, 2012, 2013), especially in countries that have been exposed to a debate about these issue, and that have a longer experience of dealing with such issues as public questions. However, there is no doubt that formal agencies of control are better equipped to "discover" the kind of criminal behaviour that is more often committed by those who live in the most marginal sectors of society, because they do engage in the more "obvious" criminal activity, such as street crime and crimes of violence.

In this respect, the case of England and Wales, studied by David J. Smith (1997) in the same volume edited by Tonry, is interesting because it represents – as also France, to a certain extent – a case that is intermediate between the other European countries and the United States, in the sense that processes of criminalization not only converge around nationalities but, and even more so, around ethnic attribution. A *leitmotiv* of Smith's contribution was in fact the question of why two groups who were supposedly equally discriminated against in the British case, i.e. Afro-Caribbeans and Black Africans on the one hand, and the various South Asian groups on the other, contributed in such a different way to processes of criminal participation and therefore criminalization, with the Afro-Caribbean group markedly outdoing the other immigrant group and whites (to the point that the likelihood of being in prison for them was seven times the probability of white or South Asian people, an overrepresentation very similar to that of African Americans in the US). Once again, "second generations" were those particularly involved in criminal participation. David Smith in his conclusion hypothesized that it may be a mix of "labelling and deviance amplification" together with "rising crime rates among the second generation of young people whose parents had migrated from the West Indies" (1997: 173) which interacted in producing a higher level of criminalization. However, how should we explain such "rising crime rates", especially considering that the previous Afro-Caribbean generation was considered to be especially law abiding (Rex and Moore 1967)? Smith makes an interesting comment that "the difference may possibly indicate [...] that the outgoing and integrative strategy initially adopted by migrants from the Caribbean was met by rejection leading to conflict, which the more separatist and inward-looking strategy of South Asians tended to avoid" (1997: 177). In other words, Indians, Bangladeshis or Pakistanis would have been wiser to the ruses of authoritarian post-colonial regimes and would have known better than to trust the promises of freedom, participation and democracy coming from the British authorities and their educational and social agencies. This way they were able to avoid conflict. Afro-Caribbeans instead (perhaps more credulous and naïve, or more staunchly pro-democratic?) would have believed in such promises and, meeting with the harsh realities of discrimination and racism, would have developed a sense of frustration and rebellion that would take them to a path of violence and crime (according to mechanisms predicted by anomie theory, from Merton to Young [2003, 2007] or by defiance theory [Sherman 1993]). After all, the explanation of the differences between first and second generations in the United States was not all that different. In her contribution to Bucerius and Tonry's new (2014) volume, Alpa Parmar goes back to this debate. She reports on the discussion between Fitzgerald's demographic argument (1995), which would explain Asians' lower rate of offending and criminalization based on their demographic profile, and indeed Smith's, based in culture and family structure (Parmar 2014: 345–8). However, she also points out that Asians' representation in rates of offending and criminalization has been increasing since the mid-1990s especially in connection with the increasing preoccupation with Muslim minorities (Bosworth and Guild 2008; Dauvergne 2008; Aliverti 2012, 2013; McCulloch and Pickering 2012; Gibney 2013, Kaufman 2013, Melossi 2013a,b,c,d).

The issue of blacks' criminalization in the UK was also the crux of a famous polemic between Stuart Hall's Birmingham School and the so-called "New Realists", between the 1970s and 1980s. Stuart Hall, together with Chas Critcher, Tony Jefferson, John Clarke and Brian Roberts, in 1978 had published *Policing the Crisis: Mugging, the State, and Law and Order*, where they criticized what they saw as the exaggerated and racist reporting of black criminality in the British tabloids. With reference to the dramatic increase of "mugging" in the 1970s, they suggested that official crime rates were employed as a useful form of scapegoating during economic crises (such as in the 1970s!), in order to draw the public's attention away from real problems. It was once again an issue of "labelling" and constructing the archetypical black male mugger. So, Stuart Hall together with Paul Gilroy, both at the Birmingham Centre for Contemporary Cultural Studies, argued that the higher levels of crime among the British black population were constructed, built by the joint efforts of formal social control apparatuses together with politicians and the media – and with a hefty contribution from the racism prevalent within police forces (Gilroy 1987). On the contrary, the "Left-Realist" perspective (Lea and Young 1984) argued that all the factors mentioned by Hall and Gilroy may certainly have been at work but that this came together with the increased levels of frustration experienced by certain ethnic minorities, contributing therefore to a higher level of offending. (Of course, one should note that this too is predicted by labelling theory, especially in Lemert's "secondary deviation" version, and it makes agencies of social control more, not less, culpable, in so far as they push those who are already marginalized by society further into the misery of crime and self-hatred.)

The case of Sweden, studied by Peter L. Martens (1997), had shown that both first and "second generation" immigrants produced higher (official) crime rates than "indigenous Swedes" but that "second generation" immigrants had lower crime rates than first generation ones, a finding that in 1997 Martens explained based on the hypothesis that such "lower rates may be a consequence of Swedish social welfare policy" (Martens 1997: 183), a social welfare which would have had a sort of "protective" effect. Would that effect still hold faced with the "riots" that developed in Stockholm in the spring of 2013? According to Barker (2013), Husby – the neighbourhood of Stockholm that was at the centre of the riots – should certainly not be confused with "hyperghettos of absolute deprivation", as Wacquant (2006) had already reminded us in his comparison of American ghettos and French *banlieues*. However, the Swedish rhetoric, and reality of the welfare state, *Folkhemmet*, the people's home (Barker 2013), seems to be based in contradictory concepts of demos and ethnos, where the latter is obviously exposed to the dangers of xenophobia and racism (Barker 2013; Ugelvik 2013).

Is there indeed something in common in a history that runs from the riots in American ghettos in the 1960s through the European "uprisings" (Newburn et al. 2011)? From Brixton in 1981 to the French *banlieues* in 2005 (Lagrange and Oberti 2006)? From the widespread English riots of 2011 to Husby in 2013? As Jock Young (2003) had already noted, a common thread seems to be found in the so-called "second generation" status of many of these young people, their fight for dignity and membership, even before work, and therefore directed against the main forces behind exclusion, i.e. the police and "racial profiling", in short, racism.[5]

Also, Josine Junger-Tas noted, again for the case of the Netherlands, that "disparities [in crime participation] appear to result largely from the unfavourable economic, social, and legal position of ethnic minorities" (Junger-Tas 1997: 257). In her book of a few years later, as we have seen, Joanne van der Leun (2003) addresses the specific situation of "illegal immigrants". Van der Leun recognizes at the outset what each migrant knows very well by experience: there are many types of "illegality" and the boundaries between "legality" and "illegality" are fuzzy and porous. In a way not too dissimilar from the Swedish case, according to van der Leun, a strong affinity exists between a strong welfare state and obstacles to the incorporation of illegal immigrants. In the more "corporatist" societies, where there is a "protected labour market" (van der Leun 2003: 24), the issue is not the favour enjoyed by "second generations", purportedly treated like everybody

---

[5]About the London 2011 riots see the *Guardian*-LSE 2011 study (Parmar 2014: 350–1). Based on these elements, an easy prediction is that Southern Europe will be next in such a chain of events.

else, but the disfavour accorded to "illegal" "first" generations – a situation that would make the experience of the Netherlands and of Southern Europe quite similar (on this see also Engbersen et al. 2014). Van der Leun also finds, as it has been shown in a number of American studies (Sullivan 1989), that the boundaries between (marginal) work, illegal and downright criminal work, and welfare, are much less clear than one would otherwise imagine. Both hypotheses that may be formulated about illegal migrants' behaviour are to a certain extent true: the "deterrence hypothesis", according to which undocumented migrants for the very reason of being undocumented will tend to keep a low profile and avoid attracting the attention of the police with deviant behaviour, and the "opportunity hypothesis", according to which the lack of legitimate opportunities will push undocumented migrants toward downright criminal behaviour. If it is generally true that the majority of undocumented are able to stay away from criminal behaviour – so much so that most illegal migrants are apprehended not because of crimes they have committed but because of illegalities of a different nature, such as violations of immigration laws or other minor illegalities – it is also true that the reduced opportunity structure that they can rely on offers crime as one among the (few) choices. In subsequent research, van der Leun together with Leerkes and Engbersen (Leerkes et al. 2012) dubbed this "the marginalization thesis", i.e. the criminogenetic influence of a compression of conventional life chances owing to both increased legislative tightness and increased repression, a paradoxical effect of increased controls (predicted, however, by labelling theory).

Police and migrants

A further interesting aspect of van der Leun's volume, and research, is about the interaction of migrants with the police (2003: 96–7), where she seems to confirm a more general finding of police research, i.e. that "police officers tend to see themselves as crime fighters and safety keepers", therefore controlling "illegal immigrants" is not the kind of thing they like to do. However, as in Egon Bittner's famous and groundbreaking account of "peace keeping" on skid-row (1967), the cumbersome intricacies of migrants' police controls in Europe make it so that the control of migration is a sort of background resource for the police that may be used at will if and when they think that may be useful. If then a Northern African-looking young man crosses the centre of the university area in Bologna at six o'clock in the morning he will probably be perceived as somebody who is going to work and nothing will be asked of him, but if the same event were to take place a couple of hours earlier, then the likelihood that he will be stopped and searched, looking for drugs or "drug money", will be much higher, as is shown in Giulia Fabini's research of the interaction between migrants and the city police in Bologna (Fabini 2014). This is an important reflection because, as we have seen, most of the contributions to Tonry's volume (1997) make the point that *police statistics* signal a higher contribution of foreigners to criminal activity and then, usually, they add, a bit like Mark Antony speaking of Brutus over Caesar's body, "yet, they [the police] are men and women of honour", meaning, they do not discriminate, not intentionally at least. However, as one of the Bologna city police officers interviewed by Fabini states, "prejudice has become a work tool", which is a bit the same as when David J. Smith (1997: 170) writes, "it can be argued, for example, that the high police stop rate of black people is 'justified' by results (reported offenses, arrests, and prosecutions)". However, as Bernard Harcourt has carefully explained in *Against Prediction* (2007), it is at the same time also the necessary premise of such results! According to Harcourt, "racial profiling" may actually have the effect of increasing rather than decreasing the overall crime rate and produces what he calls a "ratchet effect" on the prison population, a wrench that keeps tightening in one direction and one only. So, the overrepresentation of migrants and minorities in the prison cells of Europe (in the case of migrants) and America (in the case of minorities) closely mirrors their overrepresentation in police stops. In other words, police stops would be nothing more than the start of a complex processing machine, and obviously, the higher the input, the higher the output!

In fact, moving now to France,[6] Fabien Jobard and René Lévy conducted a study on police stops (Jobard and Lévy 2009). They adopted a very innovative methodological strategy, in which, at five much-trafficked Paris subway stations, they observed the number and kind of passers-by who were selected by the police to be stopped, and even interviewed them subsequently (but away from the eyes of the police) in order to elicit further information. They found that the overrepresentation of blacks and Arabs *vis à vis* whites among the young males controlled by the police was between two and fifteen times according to the site. As young people from French minorities have been chanting in the streets, riffing on the famous motto of the French revolution, "*liberté, egalité, fraternité, mais pas dans les citées*".[7] Likewise, in my own survey of (regular) migrant men

---

[6] One has to note, however, that, outside of the English-speaking countries, police research is extremely difficult to do because police forces, especially national police forces, such as the Italian one, are particularly hostile to lending themselves to be researched. On the French case, see also Body-Gendrot and Wihtol de Wenden (2003) and, more recently, Body-Gendrot (2014).

[7] I owe this to Nathalie Rostain's thesis (Rostain 2013: 115). "*Citées*", "cities", is the name given in jargon to the marginal neighbourhoods of large French cities. Body-Gendrot (2014) maintains that young people from the "*citées*" tend to identify with other youth from the same environment rather than with larger ethnic or racial groups. They also complain of their relationship with the police as "a fundamental problem of their relationship to the state" (Body-Gendrot 2014: 709).

in the Italian Region of Emilia-Romagna, I found that the likelihood of being stopped (on foot) by the police was for foreign males ten times higher than for Italians (Melossi 1999, 2010b: 454, Crocitti 2014: 810–11). This, amidst a wide discretionary behaviour that, also in the Netherlands, is well aware of "the paradox of law enforcement in immigrant communities", as Kirk et al. (2011) called it in their research in New York immigrant communities, i.e. the fact that, as a Dutch police officer states, "the whole issue of foreigners is not so interesting to me. I am working in a neighbourhood with large numbers of immigrants. If I start to take a role as someone who chases illegal immigrants, I can shake it" (van der Leun 2003: 97).[8] This "paradox of law enforcement" seems to me to be but a specific aspect of a larger "legal" paradox about the enforcement of migration law, i.e. the fact that the stricter the civil and criminal rules about illegal immigration, the greater the difficulties for migrants in finding a "peaceful" "incorporation", as van der Leun calls it, into the host society. With the insertion becoming increasingly harder, the push toward forms of nonconformist, deviant or even criminal incorporation becomes more and more likely, and so too the processes of criminalization of the migrants: because of secondary deviation, the assumption by the migrants of deviant or criminal roles follows (see also Lynch and Simon's research below). Therefore, what started under the pretence of protecting the "indigenous" public comes home to roost as an increased danger of criminal behaviour and penalization, for the migrants but also for the whole of the host society. Instead, where migrants are able to "pass" without much ado – as used to be the case in the United States before Arizona-type laws – they may insert themselves in the perhaps marginal but legal economy, making a living without endangering themselves and or their neighbour. This is after all but a specific instantiation of the larger phenomenon that Dane Archer and Rosemary Gartner (1984) called, as we have seen, "brutalization theory", a situation, in fact, where the harshness of the penal reaction to deviance or indeed of governmental action more in general has the effect of preaching to the public and therefore also to would-be criminals, that the violent and unbound exercise of one's sense of right is indeed a legitimate and reasonable way of tackling conflict. In a similar way, in the case of the United States, Sang Hea Kil and Cecilia Menjívar (2006) draw on "brutalization theory" to show how the militarized border between the US and Mexico creates an environment that breeds violence as a legitimate response to undocumented migration, a situation in which patriotism, vigilantism, racism and securitarism end up legitimating violence at the border, both by public and private "security" forces, and by criminal gangs that find people smuggling an increasingly lucrative activity.

This particular set of relationships has emerged quite clearly also in non-traditional immigration countries, such as Italy and Spain. As Kitty Calavita (2005) has shown in

---

[8] On the American case see also Engel and Swartz (2014).

her brilliant comparative analysis of the situation in Italy and Spain, immigration laws seem to "welcome" immigrants exclusively as workers, their legal status contingent on temporary work permits that are difficult to get because of cumbersome and byzantine procedures. These laws therefore limit immigrants' ability to put down roots by denying them permanent residence. Immigrants are in fact useful as "others" who are willing, or compelled, to work, under conditions and for wages that locals largely shun and that are part of a substantially "post-Fordist" setting of social and economic circumstances. The main effect of such unfriendly legal procedures is in fact – besides the obvious Darwinian consequence of selecting the sturdiest, the most adventurous, innovative and therefore the most deviant – that of creating an environment within which most migrants are obliged to take the most problematic and marginal jobs, from seasonal harvesting to construction work, from home care for the old and the disabled to precarious health industry jobs, from the lower-end of sex work to downright criminal occupations in the illegal economy. Such marginalization on the job market – Calavita shows – produces, and is at the same time a product of, the concomitant processes of "racialization" and "criminalization". Who is inferior in the job market must belong in an inferior ethnicity and if one belongs in an inferior ethnicity how could he or she aspire to a good job? At the same time, it is clear that those who have "inferior jobs" and who belong in "inferior races" will very probably have "criminal propensities" and in any case should be policed and controlled much more intensely. And we have seen how one of the by-products of "racial" or "ethnic" profiling is indeed a higher level of criminalization. But those who are criminal could never aspire to better jobs, of course, and so on, in a thoroughly vicious circle of work marginalization, racialization and criminalization that, in the case of Southern (but not only) European migrants is a substantial replica of what has been happening for decades in the case of ethnic minorities in the United States (Menjívar and Abrego 2012: 1404).

Migrants' self-reports and control theory

Because of what we have called "the double dark number of foreign crime", many researchers have come to the reasonable conclusion that a useful research strategy on the issue of migrants' and non-migrants' participation in deviant and criminal activities may be the use of self-report surveys. These are surveys where a sample of the migrant and non-migrant youth population (usually in schools) are asked to report on their behaviour and also on a number of other social, demographic and opinion aspects, useful to try to reconnect with statements on self-reported deviance. This type of study was most famously initiated by sociologist Travis Hirschi in the United

States in connection with what he called "control theory", the idea, that is, that motivation to commit crimes depends on the interaction between a "natural" tendency to break the law (in a world imagined as an association of Hobbesian actors), and the degree of "control" that society is able to exert on these actors through fundamental social institutions such as the family and the school. Hirschi believed in fact that what is in need of explanation is not so much criminal behaviour as what detains us from engaging in criminal behaviour, which he sees as the net of "social bonds" within which our socialization unfolds. In his pioneering study, Hirschi had already come to the conclusion that, in the case of ethnic minorities, labelling theory – which, generally speaking, he adamantly opposed – was however "particularly persuasive" as "an explanation of differential official rates" of crime (1969: 78). He further stated that "[i]t is of the essence of social class that it can create differences in reward where none exists in talent, that it can impose differences in punishment where none exists in obedience to rules" (1969: 82).

According to Martin Killias' reconstruction, recent European self-report surveys have, however, shown that "immigrant juveniles usually admit, during interviews, more offences than do natives. This is true especially for violent offences" (2011: 5). He then goes on to mention research done in Germany, France, Switzerland and "most of the Western European countries that participated in the second international self-report study" (Junger-Tas et al. 2010, 2011). At the same time, David Smith reports a British study by Graham and Bowling (1995) according to which there would have been "no differences in rates of self-reported offending between black and white youths" (Smith 1997: 171)[9]. Also in several self-report delinquency studies we conducted in the Italian Region of Emilia-Romagna (Melossi et al. 2009; Crocitti 2011; Melossi et al. 2011), we found no evidence of a higher frequency or seriousness of self-reported deviance among young first or second generation immigrants compared to Italians (furthermore, whereas the results for second generation minors were very similar to the results for Italian minors, first generation children had a slightly lesser chance of involvement in deviant behaviour). At the same time, both for Italian and immigrant respondents, self-reported deviant behaviour appeared to be strongly related to conflicts and problems with authority figures, in school and especially within the family, in accordance with Hirschi's original theory.

Those studies of self-reported youth behaviour that find a higher relevance for migrant and minority groups usually emphasize the role of violent offences, i.e. more serious deviance committed by older youths. Once again, one wonders about the role that may be played by secondary deviation, something that is relevant also for the differences found between first and second generations, with the latter usually

---

[9]See also Parmar (2014: 328), Junger (1989) and Sharp and Budd (2005).

showing higher levels of deviance than the former. That the process of social integration should take place at the same time as an increase in deviant behaviour is less
surprising than one would expect. I think we should reiterate the two dimensions
that have a bearing on second generations' destiny, so to speak (and that may apply
to those at the older end of the youth spectrum to a greater extent than to younger
ones). On the one hand, their increased deviance is probably also the product of racism and discrimination, because they are generally asked to integrate within a
society – and in specific neighbourhoods – that offer a mirror-image of their selves
which is marked by exclusion and inferiorization. At the same time, second generation
youths are more willing to take chances and break with the hyperconformism both of
their families and of European societies. They may be willing, in other words, to make
innovative choices once they consider themselves to be full participants in the local
society, according to the promises of equality that we have seen to be characteristic of
(most) countries of immigration. However, such "innovative choices" may be met in a
widely differentiated manner, as was noted by William Chambliss as long ago as 1973
in his famous article about the "saints" and the "roughnecks". What applied to the
roughnecks in terms of social class will certainly be true for the migrant youth group
too (given that, demographically, immigration may very well be considered as a sort of
mass import of a whole new section of the working class in a given society[10]).

In the case of second generations, I do not think we can discount – as Sampson notes
for the United States – the "drifting"[11] character of their path to integration within the
larger "indigenous" group they are entering.[12] At the same time I do not think we can
underestimate – beyond the rhetoric of "culture conflict" *à la* Sellin (1938) – the role
played by their specific kind of insertion into native society. Theirs is generally the

---

[10]I mean it literally: in our studies, half of the "Italian" students' fathers could be described as
"middle class" and about a quarter as "working class": those proportions were exactly inverted
for the "migrant" students' fathers and even more so if we look at the mothers' occupation
(Melossi et al. 2011: 38–9).

[11]In Matza's sense (1964).

[12]The different condition of first and second generations is however something that should be
kept completely separate from the issue of so-called "unaccompanied minors", who certainly are
"first generation" but who also suffer from lack of documentation – until at least when (some of
them) are taken in charge by social services. They are in fact the category which, at least in Italy,
has been feeding juvenile penal institutions in large percentages, and who seem to be generally
destined to a situation of exclusion, marginality and deviance. Their condition is drastically different from those first generations who came with their families or at least one of the parents and
who are therefore protected both by that relationship and by the moral and customary norms of
their original culture, often stricter than the one of the receiving country.

insertion of the one who already belongs in terms of language, habits and customs, but, nevertheless may find himself or herself without citizenship – maybe with their parents' citizenship, the citizenship of a place they have never seen and the language of which they cannot speak.[13] And all of this without even mentioning the peculiar spectacle that the host society often offers them and their parents. The label of "Balotelli generation" – referring to black Italian (citizen) soccer champion Mario Balotelli who would often enter a stadium in Italy to see giant banners displaying the message "THERE ARE NO ITALIAN BLACKS" – could not be more appropriate![14] Obviously this may mean, as was observed by Jock Young (2003), a very strong cultural and emotional stress. It is difficult to discount in fact the peculiarly negative effects of the collective labelling of whole social groups and it may very well be that such negative effects may show up more openly once an older youth starts to be more autonomous from his or her family. It may very well be at the same time that the prejudice and the racial and national profiling may cause some of these young people, once they are older – and as the idea of "secondary deviation" predicts – to do their best to show that they are indeed up to the image that is pictured of them.

Lack of documentation and crime in a period of crisis

Generally speaking, undocumented migrants are people who entered legally (for instance on a tourist visa) or who acquired the proper documents for work, but subsequently lost the qualifications to stay – a particularly critical problem in the economic crisis that started in 2008, given that work is one of the premises for maintaining the permit to stay legally in an EU member state. The problem

---

[13]According to Caritas (2010), there were in 2010 in Italy almost 600,000 "foreigners" born in Italy!

[14]The same has happened with several other soccer players in Italy; Balotelli has, however, the distinction of being the most famous, and an Italian citizen! As a butt for racist remarks and "jokes" he was more recently replaced by Kashetu "Cécile" Kyenge, an Italian citizen of Congolese origins and the first black person to become, on 28 April 2013, a Minister ("of Integration") in an Italian government, an experience that ended quite soon, on 22 February 2014, with the end of the government of which she was part. The obvious reference, in terms of analysis, should be to the work of British black intellectual Paul Gilroy who, working from Stuart Hall's Centre for Contemporary Cultural Studies at Birmingham University in the 1980s, authored the epoch-making book *Ain't No Black in the Union Jack* (Gilroy 1987).

is of course that the condition of being without documents places the foreign citizen within a set of conditions and constrictions that increase all the risk factors for criminal behaviour enormously (besides making them more visible to official agencies of control).

In other words, the problem of the relationship between the documented status and the risk of deviant behaviour is first of all a legislative and more generally normative one which concerns many country members of the European Union, because of the cumbersome nature of entry procedures. Especially in the case of unskilled labour (which is the kind of labour largely on demand), until the beginning of the economic crisis those who aspired to come and work in Europe would try to enter, or "overstay", by every means possible in order to play thereafter a game of wait and see. The hunger for labour of European societies was such in fact that, sooner or later, some kind of individual or collective provision would eventually be enacted[15] – thereby recognizing the rational, albeit unlawful, strategy of the migrants, not to mention the importance of their contribution to the welfare of the country. However, this situation is such as to create a sort of "gap" in the migrant's biography, when he or she has no chance to work legally, therefore making them more likely to become prey to a variety of illegal or downright criminal "occupations". This problem may of course acquire different characteristics according to the specific national legislation and may be quite different also if applied to so-called "economic" migrants or to asylum seekers.

The nature of the problems has somewhat changed with the economic crisis that started in 2008 and which has greatly increased migrants' unemployment.[16] According to a report by the International Organization for Migration (IOM) (2010), the economic crisis has had quite an impact on migration flows in Europe, especially in those EU countries "that experienced large inflows of labour migrants in the pre-crisis period, countries for which labour migration is the main immigration

---

[15]Routinely, Italian studies have shown that at least half of the regular, documented male immigrants witnessed to the fact that they found themselves without documentation for a period, whereas most women came to Italy based on family reunifications asked for by those very immigrants (Melossi 1999; Ambrosini 2009). Oxfam estimated that close to 90 per cent of asylum seekers came to Europe illegally (Morrison 2000: 26; Oxfam 2005: 35; Lee 2011: 57).

[16]It is a well-established fact of criminological research on the connections between criminal behaviour and economic change – starting with Thorsten Sellin's time-honoured pioneering effort occasioned by the 1930s crisis (Sellin 1937) – that, in a situation of deep recession, criminal behaviour tends to increase, considering it on the side of criminal motivation, but tends at the same time to decline, considering it instead on the side of criminal opportunities, which become fewer and fewer.

stream. Ireland, Spain, and the UK all registered falling net migration". Furthermore, "although emigration levels of foreign national residents increased in some EU countries during the economic downturn, it is unclear to what extent many of these emigrants actually returned to their home country", especially the non-EU migrants, because of the foreseeable difficulty in re-entering the EU. In any case, the same IOM (2010) report states:

the employment situation of migrant workers, especially of nationals of non-EU countries, deteriorated more rapidly than that of natives during the economic crisis. The increase in the unemployment rates for foreign workers (including those from EU countries) compared to those for native workers between 2008 and 2009 was most marked in Estonia, Spain, Portugal, Latvia, Ireland, France, and Austria. Foreign workers from non-EU countries were particularly affected by worsening employment conditions. While unemployment rates for nationals of other EU countries increased by 2.8 percentage points between 2008 and 2009, those for non-EU nationals rose by 5 per cent during the same period. The difference may be partly explained by the high concentration of non-EU foreign workers in sectors with high cyclical demand such as construction, retail, and hospitality.

Finally,

the irregular migrant population is likely to have increased during the downturn but less because of new irregular inflows, and more because of migrants overstaying their visas or permits and moving to find work in the grey economy. Many migrant workers have lost their jobs, during the recession, but have not returned home. In countries where migrants' entitlements to social welfare benefits are limited, there may have been an increase in the number of migrants working in the informal economy as a result of the crisis.

Young Europeans, especially from Southern Europe but also from Ireland and the UK, now join former migrants returning home to countries such as Argentina and Brazil.[17] A report by the European Commission (2009) to the European Parliament showed that the rate of unemployment for third-country nationals (documented, of course) had gone from 13.6 per cent in 2008 to 18.9 per cent in 2009 (8.4 per cent for nationals) in the then EU-27. The consequence has been that,

overall immigration to developed countries has slowed sharply as a result of the economic crisis, bringing to a virtual halt the rapid growth in foreign-born populations over the past three decades. In the two years since the onset of the global economic

---

[17]See articles in *The Guardian* on migrations and crisis: www.theguardian.com/world/2011/dec/22/young-europeans-emigrate-argentina-jobs (accessed 10 February 2015).

crisis, temporary workers flows, business migration, and 'unregulated' flows such as illegal immigration and free movement within certain parts of the European Union have experienced the largest decreases. (Papademetriou et al. 2010: 1)

Most amazing is the case of Mexico, where during the crisis the number of those who were coming back or migrating to Mexico from the United States or Spain overcame the number of people leaving Mexico.

This is probably connected also to the planned attitude of hostility that has been created by many European governments and political forces in both its more and less official aspects, such as, for instance in Italy, the passing of laws (in the process of being repealed at time of writing) that criminalized the lack of documentation *per se*. For instance, according to the Italian research institute ISMU, there has been a definite slowdown of new immigrant entries into Italy in 2010, about 100,000 fewer than in 2007, the last pre-crisis year (minus 40 per cent).[18] It is interesting to note also that the percentage of foreigners in prison has slightly declined in Italy – by 2.6 per cent between 2010 and 2012.[19] Exactly as happened in the United States in the 1920s, first with the introduction of admission quotas and then especially with the Great Depression of 1929, the changed scenario may be conducive to a shift of attention from first generations of migrants coming into the country, to the integration of so-called "second generations", the children of those who made it in.

The overrepresentation of non-EU citizens in prison

It is a matter of fact that, as shown in Table 3.1, in Europe (and particularly in the European countries that first created the European Community) the overrepresentation of non-EU citizens in prison is many times their share of the general population (see also Melossi 2003a, 2005).[20]

---

[18] 16th Report on Migrations by ISMU (*La Repubblica*, 13 December 2010). This was very much still the case in 2013.

[19] ISMU, newsletter of 8 March 2012.

[20] Furthermore, also in Europe there is a whole specialized sector of internment and detention for migrants, mostly outside the penal system, which has given birth to a reality often referred to with the moniker "Fortress Europe". See the special section of the *European Journal of Criminology* dedicated to immigration detention in Europe, edited by Leonidas K. Cheliotis (2013). See also the work of Ana Aliverti (2013) and Giuseppe Campesi (2013).

Table 3.1 Overrepresentation of foreigners in EU prison systems

	Percent of foreigners in prison pop.[1]	Percent of foreigners /foreigners extra-EU in general pop.[2]	Estimate of the rate of overrepresentation[3]
Austria	48.6	11.2/6.7	4.3–7.2
Belgium	44.2	11/3.9	4–11.3
Bulgaria	2	.6/.4	3.3–5
Croatia	5.7	.8[4]	7.1
Cyprus	53.8	20/7.4	2.7–7.3
Czech Republic	9.1	4/2.6	2.3–3.5
Denmark	26.8	6.4/4	4.2–6.7
Estonia	39.9	16/14.9	1.9–2.7
Finland	14.5	3.4/2.1	4.3–6.9
France	17.5	5.9/3.8	3–4.6
Germany	27.1	9.1/5.7	3–4.8
Greece	63.2	8.6/7.2	7.3–8.8
Hungary	3.5	2.1/0.8	1.7–4.4
Ireland	14.5	10.6/2.1	1.4–6.9
Italy	34.4	8.1/5.7	4.2–6
Latvia	1.3	16.3/16	0.08
Lithuania	1.2	.7/0.6	1.7–2
Luxemburg	72.2	43.8/5.9	1.6–12.2
Malta	40.3	4.9	8.2
Netherlands	24.6	4.2/2	5.9–12.3

(Continued)

Table 3.1 (Continued)

	Percent of foreigners in prison pop.[1]	Percent of foreigners /foreigners extra-EU in general pop.[2]	Estimate of the rate of overrepresentation[3]
Poland	0.7	.1/.06	7–11.7
Portugal	18.3	4.2/3.2	4.4/5.7
Romania	0.6	.2/.16	3/3.7
Slovakia	2	1.3/0.3	1.5–6.7
Slovenia	10.7	4.2/3.9	2.5–2.7
Spain	31.6	12/6.9	2.6–4.6
Sweden	30.5	6.8/3.9	4.5–7.8
United Kingdom	12.8[5]	7.6/3.9[6]	1.7–3.3

[1] Latest data available from the International Centre for Prison Studies, King's College, University of London, between 2011 and beginning months of 2014, according to the country.

[2] Percentage of foreigners/foreigners from countries outside the EU-28 in the general population (on 1 January 2012; source: EUROSTAT).

[3] I divided the number in the first column by both numbers in the second column: the result is the estimate in the third column, somewhere in between the two numbers. Why is that? Because we do not have a distinction of the percentages of inmates according to whether they are simply foreigners or foreigners from outside of the EU, information that we do have about the general population of foreigners. Most inmates are from countries outside the EU, so the second term of the estimate is probably more precise. There is, however, one important exception to such a rule of thumb, the fact that the situation has changed with the admission of Romania to the EU because the number of Romanians incarcerated in several countries is substantial.

[4] Data for Croatia are from 2008 and do not report information on where foreigners are from.

[5] Data for England and Wales.

[6] Data for the UK.

Analysis of this table could certainly be a research task in itself. For now, it will be enough to notice that there are *grosso modo* four groups of countries among the EU-28. A first group is what we could call the large, traditional immigration countries. Especially in former colonial countries, such as France or the UK, there may be naturalized citizens, often from former colonies, who are in prison because of social mechanisms not unlike those that lead to foreigners' imprisonment, but obviously they do not show up in foreigners' statistics (for instance, the UK overrepresentation of migrants is one of the lowest among the EU countries, but we have seen that the overrepresentation of Afro-Caribbeans in UK prisons is equal to seven times the likelihood of white or South Asian people to be in prison, an overrepresentation very similar to that of African Americans in the United States [Smith 1997; Agozino 2003; for France see Tournier 1997]). In small central European countries, and especially in Belgium and Luxembourg, a substantial number of inmates come from neighbouring EU countries, which explains in part the very wide estimate. In Southern European countries, in contrast, what is characteristic is their high level of undocumented migrants (Calavita 2005), caused by the almost impossible task of immigrating legally, especially for reasons of work. Particularly in these countries, the criminal justice system provides the only type of institutional "care" and "welfare" available to "criminal" migrants, who are almost always undocumented and therefore devoid of political or social citizenship (paradoxically, criminal migrants in prisons enjoy standards that may be higher than those doled out to undocumented migrants held in *ad-hoc* detention centres). One should note, however, that the overrepresentation in Spain (Brandariz García and Monclús Masó, 2015) – which, just before the economic crisis, competed with the United States and Germany as the most sought-after world-wide destination for migrants – has been regularly declining, given that the increase in the foreign prison population has not kept pace with the increase in the general foreign population. Finally, there are Eastern European countries, where, generally speaking, there are almost no migrants and therefore no migrants in prison. As a matter of fact, these countries often have higher imprisonment rates. Many are emigrant countries, such as Poland and Romania, much as Italy might have been, for instance, until about half a century ago.

The social mechanisms that may produce such data, in the European case, are the most various, from the high visibility of migrants' crime *vis à vis* the extremely low visibility of other kinds of crime ('crime in the street' vs. 'crime in the suites'!), from the specific crimes that only migrants can commit, to the public and legislative prejudice against them, from the discriminatory behaviour of many public institutions, to the migrants' deprivation of the fundamental right to have an efficient defence and the impossibility of applying to migrants a host of pre- and after-trial benefits that keep natives out of prison but that railroad foreigners into detention (aspects that we have at least partially summarized in the concept of "double dark number of foreign crime"). Furthermore, all of this is limited to the functioning of social control apparatuses. It does not even begin to take into consideration the basic issue of the social, economic and cultural condition of disadvantage from which many migrants start.

Europe, a "land of immigration": border "security" in Fortress Europe

The whole conundrum of immigration is no longer a national but rather eminently a European, and specifically an EU, issue. As already pointed out, there is a paradox at work here, because policies of restriction, which are invoked on the grounds also of defending natives from migrants' crime, end up creating the preconditions for a higher criminalization of migrants (which is both a harsher social reaction but also at the same time a higher level of criminal behaviour by the migrants). The difficulties with treating the whole issue of migration seriously is but one (not secondary) aspect, I believe, of the more general difficulty that the European Union has with policies about matters of common import, that go deeply into the cultural spheres of the various European countries and that are at this point impossible to treat as mere "international" issues. However, the lack of a genuine European public sphere makes this kind of public conversation very difficult.

At the same time, it also seems to me that, beyond this overall difficulty, we are facing a more specific "socio-criminological difficulty". As mentioned, it has to do with a style of criminological thinking that has gone back to an ancillary vision of the discipline that ignores the wisdom of 1960s sociology of deviance, which showed that one of the (unintended?) results of greater repression is, at least in part, more intense and committed criminal behaviour. Such "criminological difficulty" would not have had such a devastating effect, however, were it not for an utter lack of ideas, conceptions and imagination on the issue of immigration. Whereas recent developments in EU law have supposedly "communitarized" the matter of immigration, from the Treaty of Amsterdam (1999) all the way to the Treaty of Lisbon (2009) and the most recent "Stockholm Programme", such developments – within the rather depressing status of the whole European enterprise lately – have by and large remained on paper, with the various national governments bickering bitterly among themselves about the fundamentals of the immigration phenomenon. The need for immigrants, *vis à vis* the incredibly low level of demographic reproduction in Europe, way below stability, has been consistently underestimated, compelling would-be migrants to try to come undocumented or often under the guise of asylum seekers, and thus exposing themselves and their families to the risk of being criminalized in one way or another.

The political framework that has caused such incredibly restrictive and myopic policies is based on the premise that each of the European countries jealously guards its own competence on the subject of immigration and is quite forgetful of the communitarization of the matter! The easy use of immigration as a scapegoat, a kind of balloon thrown back and forth between fast-rising extreme right groups, which have made xenophobia and racism their *raison d'être*, and the moderate majorities of centre-right and centre-left, which exploit such dangerous issues for opportunistic electoral gain, has again become one of the mainstays of European politics. This has of course also made the fortune of all kinds of marginal or downright criminal economic enterprises, which find in the provision of cheap undocumented immigrant labour their hope of surviving a market where they would otherwise have no hope whatsoever.

The alternative to all of this would be to move towards the basic and frank recognition of Europe as a "country of immigration" (as was done by the new German government in 1998 about Germany). Such a decision would, however, imply the need for some kind of clear concepts as to what "Europe", and more specifically the EU, is and what it stands for. It would also imply the existence of a debate over the issue, and of the procedural channels necessary to make such a debate happen. The question of migration in Europe, with all those other questions to which it is usually, rightly or wrongly, connected, such as those of security and crime, is *prima facie* the kind of issue that cannot be discussed (only) in the very many languages that characterize Europe today as a political entity. The problem in fact is transnational, and similarly transnational are the decisions and the policies to be made and implemented. To be shy about such matters simply means to give in to what is going on in many European countries today, where issues such as that of migration are not even discussed any longer in rational terms and are often the object of a localistic and para-Fascist jargon (Melossi 2005) (this in spite of the work of the courts [van Zyl Smit and Snacken 2009], such as the European Court of Human Rights and the Committee for the Prevention of Torture and, within the institutions of the European Union, the jurisprudence of the Court of Justice, which have been trying to ensure respect for the basic human rights and, among these, those of immigrants from outside of the EU).

Many years ago, the sociologist Kai Erikson (1966), in reconstructing the waywardness of seventeenth-century Massachusetts Puritans, put forward an interesting idea, according to which, through the extended public discussion of crucial instances of deviance, communities converse within themselves, about their identity and where they want to go. Likewise, I would submit that, through this crucial issue of immigration, we Europeans have been conversing for some time now about ourselves, who we are and where we want to go (Douglas 1966). The European mass-media are replete with talk about immigrants' criminal and cultural deviance; an arena where we Europeans debate about the existence, nature and essential characteristics of a European identity that appears to be very problematic indeed.

Unfortunately, if we consider the reality of today's *European* policies of migration and border control, we seem to be quite far away from the ideal of Europe, and the EU, as a "land of immigration". Katja Franko Aas (2011) has explored the nature of surveillance and crime control in connection with the new reality of global governance. Within the European Union, the coupling of surveillance and crime control has increasingly played a role in constructing a particular type of globally divided polity. This has connected with a deep transformation in our notions of citizenship, what Aas calls "hierarchies of citizenship" (Aas 2013: 28–32). As in a new version of the old Greek democracy, the category of citizenship is fragmented into an array of figures that go from the "bona fide global citizen" – as Aas calls him or her – to the regular immigrant, to the undocumented "other", a fragmentation that the traditional liberal language of citizenship has a hard time accounting for. Tomas Hammar (1990: 200) had written of "denizens" in this respect and, before him, Michael Walzer (1983: 58–9) spoke of "Athenian metics", people who would have the right to work, indefinitely or for a limited time, but no political rights.

Especially in relation to the development of detention and deportation – in many countries in specialized *ad hoc* institutions – a lively theoretical debate has ensued on the connection of this new reality with the Western legal and political tradition. Some have pointed at a historical thread that from Carl Schmitt and Hannah Arendt goes to Giorgio Agamben's idea of a "state of exception" that reduces human beings to being "bare life" within the form of "the camp" (De Genova 2002; Rahola 2003) – a trajectory somewhat akin to the one developed in criminal law by Günther Jakobs, a German professor of criminal law, who developed the notion of "criminal law for enemies" or *enemy penology* (*Feindstrafrecht*) (Krasmann 2007; Zedner 2013). Others have opposed an interpretation reconnecting instead migrants' detention to the "normality" of the history of police powers, especially on the European continent (Campesi 2013, see also Johansen 2013). Yet others have developed a conception of detention as a *de facto* punishment, framing this idea in the (questionable) neologism of "crimmigration" (Stumpf 2013) or talking about "crimes of mobility" (Aliverti 2013), or "criminalization of migrants" (Melossi 2012, 2013a,b,c,d) or, emphasizing legal aspects different from criminal law – "legal violence" (Menjívar and Abrego 2012).

As I have mentioned, most of the European efforts in organizing the area of "freedom, liberty and justice" seem to have gone into a ceaseless effort to patrol the external borders that duplicates, at the European level, what national governments have already been doing. This has also brought about forms of competition between the new-born European policing efforts and the more entrenched national policies, squabbles that would have been almost ludicrous were they not having an impact on the lives of thousands and thousands of would-be immigrants. This for instance happened in the sort of competition between Frontex (see below) and the separate bilateral Italian-Libyan efforts in patrolling the Mediterranean, which may have been one of the reasons for some of the misunderstandings between Italy and the rest of Europe in the "crisis" of 2011, when the flow of migrants landing on Italian shores in Lampedusa increased sharply and suddenly (see Giuseppe Campesi's analysis [2011] of the way in which the Euro-Mediterranean "border-control regime" has been reacting to the so-called "Arab Spring").

At the time of writing, the curtain had just been brought down on the Mare Nostrum operation ("our sea", as the Ancient Romans would call the Mediterranean). However uncouth the name, the policy was good. From November 2013 to October 2014, Italian coastguard and naval forces saved almost 150,000 people at sea, mostly coming from countries at war and therefore to be considered as refugees and asylum seekers (however, between 1,600 and 2,000 people are estimated not to have made it, having drowned in the attempt to cross[21]). In any case the operation was terminated because it was too costly, with Italy complaining that it did not receive the support it hoped for both in the management of the operation and especially later on in welcoming the hundreds of thousands of asylum seekers. In fact, in the last few months of Mare Nostrum, the Italian authorities seemed to basically encourage the migrants arrived on Italian coasts to cross Italian soil as soon as possible and ask for asylum in other European countries (where they in fact intended to go!). This in order to circumvent the so-called "Dublin[22] rule" according to which a refugee has to ask for asylum in the country of first arrival. In a sense, Italians learned from the legally unscrupulous behaviour of the migrants. A network of small entrepreneurs emerged, specialized in moving the migrants across Italian borders and toward countries north of the Alps.[23] This was probably the reason why another functionary – or perhaps the same one, with a strong appreciation for the Latin roots of Italian language – contributed to setting up a police dragnet operation across Europe, between 13 October and 26 October 2014 this time called Mos Maiorum ("the custom of ancestors"!). This operation was intended to recapture at least some of these "outlaw" migrants and asylum seekers crisscrossing the European Union after having escaped death in their countries of origin and at sea. The successor operation to Mare Nostrum was to be operation Triton, limited to patrolling a zone stretching just

---

[21]Out of 3,419 migrants who lost their lives in the Mediterranean during 2014 (estimate of the UNHCR).

[22]From the city where a number of conventions on asylum among European countries were signed.

[23]All this information is based on articles in the Italian daily newspaper *La Repubblica* that appeared between 26 August and 3 September 2014.

30 miles from Europe's coast, and now managed directly by the EU agency Frontex. On its official site, Frontex defines itself in these terms:[24]

> Schengen countries are obliged to deploy sufficient staff and resources to ensure a "high and uniform level of control" at the external borders of the Schengen area. They must also ensure that border guards are properly trained. EU and Schengen Associated Countries also assist each other with the effective application of border controls via operational cooperation, which is coordinated by the EU agency Frontex. Its main task is to augment and to add value to border control activities of the Member States. Thus the agency is also mandated to assist EU countries in raising and harmonizing border management standards with the aim of combating cross-border crime while making legitimate passage across the external border of the EU faster and easier.

A further glance at the site will show that the fight against "irregular migration" is a very large part indeed of that "cross-border crime". These policies seem today to have broad political support in Europe – even if there are increasing signs, especially in Southern Europe, that the rising preoccupations with economic difficulties are placing the question of immigration (and the related issue of crime) in second place (for instance, according to the European Report on Security coordinated by Italian sociologist Ilvo Diamanti [2012]). At the same time, it should also be made clear that the right-wing groups, which are militantly against immigrants and more inclusive immigration policies, are as vehemently opposed to the EU. And in all public opinion polls the overlapping of right-wing political alignment and enmity against both immigration and the process of "Europeanization" (so to speak), is quite consistent (Hochschild and Brown 2014). Alin M. Ceobanu (2011) has confirmed in his own research what many previous studies had already shown, i.e. that anti-immigrant attitudes – and the tendency to attribute to immigrants criminal propensities – are more common among older men, with low social capital, isolated, unemployed, and who have an affinity for right-wing organizations and ideologies. On the contrary, personal contact with immigrants, education and being a student have the opposite result.

   The fact of the matter is that there are a number of concepts of Europe. The idea, and the type of policies, which are often expressed with the moniker "Fortress Europe" belong within nationalist groups, in each European country, that, by referring to a restrictive and discriminatory policy against the migrants, invoke a "European" tradition, often based in religion and race. What I am in other words suggesting is a true divorce of a traditionalist concept of "Europe" – a concept that for many centuries has gone together with economic exploitation, racism and colonialism – and the idea instead of a specific political entity, the EU, as something to be built together, by the

---

[24]http://frontex.europa.eu/operations/roles-and-responsibilities (accessed 22 August 2014).

European peoples and the immigrants, based on premises that are indeed the opposite of those of the "European tradition". *Therefore Europe is one thing, the EU is another.* I believe that the moniker "Fortress Europe" is justified only if the former takes over the process of building the latter. But this is a matter for political and cultural struggle. It is in no way something that should be taken for granted. Europeans cannot really converse among themselves about the question of immigration without building a common house of language and culture able to sustain the public debate that would be needed. The question of a more rational and humane approach to the issue of immigration in Europe is therefore strictly intertwined with the process of making the EU itself. Immigrants are indeed those who have not only the highest stake but also the greatest ability to be part of the process and, at the same time, of the debate necessary to make it unfold (Melossi 1990, 2005).

What appears to be a true persecution of strangers in Europe – but, as we shall see in the next chapter, not only in Europe but in all countries that had been, until recently, e-migration countries – corresponds to a situation in which the rhetoric of the country of immigration has been sorely lacking, indeed the recognition of being countries of immigration at all, is still lacking. As was mentioned at the beginning of this chapter, this is no surprise coming from a constellation of statelets that have routinely solved their economic, social and political problems by sending away the best part of their younger generations, usually those for whom it was hardest to bow in front of arrogance, injustice and corruption. After all, being that the new mass of immigrants went to replenish the ranks of the lowest strata of the working class, European societies have done nothing less but treat the immigrants as they were accustomed to treat the most disadvantaged among their own – something that had become hard to do after the workers' militancy of the 1960s and 1970s. As we shall see in the next chapter, the European masters have been largely overcome, at this game of shame, by their counterparts from the Middle East, Africa and Asia.

FOUR

the importance of legal status in a globalized world

In her interview to the journal *Social Justice*, at some point Angela Davis, the African American intellectual and political activist (among other things, for the abolition of prisons), notes that,

> [t]he value of abolitionist approaches [is] most clearly visible in the global South, which has suffered structural adjustment.

And she goes on:

> More prisons are being built to catch the lives disrupted by this movement of capital. People who cannot find a place for themselves in this new society governed by capital end up going to prison. In many countries, such as South Africa and Colombia [...] deterritorialization is underway to allow agribusiness to expand, thus producing surplus populations. In Colombia, people have been removed from their land to make way for sugarcane production for the biofuel consumed by us in the West who wish to mini-mize our carbon footprint. All the people ejected from that land, who had protected its biodiversity, are being pushed into slums. It is most intense near Cali, in the western part of Colombia, where they are building the largest prison in South America—in part to catch those people who have been deprived of their land and have no source of cash. Thus, the value of abolition is clear in places now acquiring US-style prisons due to shifts in the economy. (Davis 2014: 51–2)

It is remarkable how similar is Davis' account to the one at the beginning of this book, where I quoted Marx's description of the peasants' ejection from their land in Elizabethan England. Is this simply because Davis is an unabashed Marxist? Perhaps. However, I would like the open-minded reader to entertain the idea that the expla-nation may also be that the social process described by Karl Marx for the sixteenth century is still going on in its basic features at this very time, the only difference being its scale, which is now, as the topical word enunciates, indeed "global".

The process of globalization that developed between the early 1990s and the deep "global" economic crisis that started in 2008, was accompanied by a big surge in migration movements all over the world. According to a Pew report,[1] an increasing number of migrants live in the United States and other high-income countries. Whereas one-fifth of the world's migrants live in the US, seven in ten live in other higher-income nations (those with a per capita income of at least $12,616). A general movement seems to be from middle-income countries such as India or Mexico to high-income countries, such as North American and European countries. As always with migrations, economic conditions play a central role in the flow of immigrants. Another top destination is Russia.[2] Germany is third. No country comes close to the United States, however, where the number of immigrants doubled to 46 million in 2013 from 23 million in 1990. However, the number of the foreign-born as a share of the total US population is considerably lower than in many other nations. In the United States, about 14 per cent of the population in 2013 was foreign born, less than Australia at 28 per cent, or Canada, 21 per cent. In some countries in the Persian Gulf, moreover, the vast majorities of their populations are foreign-born workers (for instance, 84 per cent of the population in the United Arab Emirates or 74 per cent in Qatar).

In other words, migratory movements particularly interested some of the hubs in international globalization and development, such as South Africa; Argentina and Brazil in South America; Israel and the Gulf Cooperation Council (namely, Bahrain, Kuwait, Oman, Qatar, Saudi Arabia and the United Arab Emirates) in the Middle East; Australia; and Asia, where it is possible to differentiate between mainly destination countries (Brunei, Hong Kong, Japan, Singapore, South Korea, Taiwan), countries with both significant immigration and emigration (Malaysia and Thailand), and mainly source countries (Bangladesh, Burma, Cambodia, China, India, Indonesia, Laos, Nepal, Pakistan, Philippines, Sri Lanka and Vietnam). In all of these magnets of migration, social processes turned out to be quite similar – and similar to those that we have already seen in the case of North America and Europe.

And yet, at the same time, each one of those developed, with peculiarities of its own, something that was expressed by social theorist Zygmunt Bauman – as Mimi Ajzenstadt and Assaf Shapira remind us in their reconstruction of the judicial construction of "otherness" in Israel – by stating that "all societies produce strangers; but each kind of society produces its own kind of strangers, and produces them in

---

[1]The report is available at: www.pewsocialtrends.org/2013/12/17/changing-patterns-of-global-migration-and-remittances/ (accessed 10 February 2015).

[2]However, one should not forget that after the dissolution of the Soviet Union many nationals of former members of the Soviet Union who found themselves in Russia at the moment of the breakdown are counted as migrants.

its own inimitable way" (Bauman 1995: 1). There seem to be, however, aspects that, outside of the centres of Western democratic capitalism, bring some of these processes to their extremes – with the new masters doing their best in order to outdo the old ones. The reduction of large segments of the population to an almost servile condition, with the ruthless suppression of basic rights, and especially of labour rights, and the corresponding construction of various forms of apartheid based in social class and "race", seem to be similar processes in all of these sites, to a greater or lesser extent.

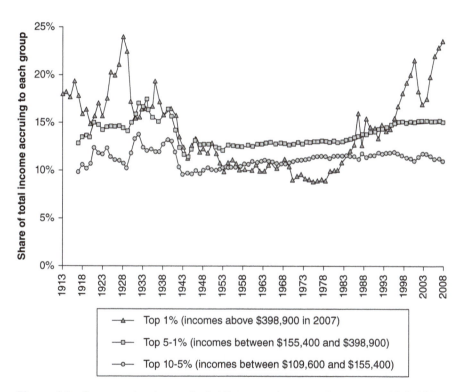

Figure 4.1 Decomposing the top decile US income share into three groups, 1913–2007

Source: Saez (2009), update to 2007 of Piketty and Saez (2003).

Income is defined as market income including capital gains.

Top 1% denotes the top percentile (families with annual income above $398,900 in 2007).

Top 5–1% denotes the next 4% (families with annual income between $155,400 and $398,900 in 2007).

Top 10–5% denotes the next 5% (bottom half of the top decide, families with annual income between $109,600 and $155,400 in 2007).

The point seems to be that, at the intersection of migration law, criminal law and the economy, a specific path to socio-economic development seems to be put in place, in motion, if you wish (see also Mezzadra and Neilson 2013: ix). All these processes happened during the high peak of globalization, between the 1990s and the crisis starting in 2007/2008 (according to country), a period called by many "neo-liberalism".

As one may see from Figure 4.1, an incredible increase in social inequality took place in this period (more generally, see Piketty 2013). There has also been a restriction on labour rights and union rights everywhere, a retreat from the construction of the welfare state or, in the American case, what we call the New Deal arrangement, the kind of society that had been built by Franklin Delano Roosevelt. Rightly David Garland in *Culture of Control* (2001) writes of "penal welfarism" and of how penal welfarism ended with the end of the welfare state.

More specifically, what I would call the creation of a pariah or outcast class, an outcast section of society (Wacquant 2006), was created in every society, according to different traditions and different realities. It is not that you always find the same people among the outcasts or among the pariahs; that changes. For instance, in the case of the United States, as we have seen, that is very much connected with race and is less connected with migration. That makes sense in terms of the history of the United States, which is a rather troubled history about race, and instead is a country in which there is pride about migration, especially migration from Europe, migration as the very "constitution" of American society. Very different is the situation in Europe and especially in Southern Europe, in which migrants have always been part of what has to be controlled. As we have seen, if you focus on the creation of national states in the nineteenth century, in most continental European countries the police was basically created for the control of mobility of three groups: the strangers, the prostitutes (women moving from place to place, town to town), and vagrants and vagabonds. Still in continental Europe today – that is certainly still the case in Italy – it is the police's business to control migration, even if it has nothing to do with crime, but with the permit to stay. So that for almost anything that has to do with their migrant status, "foreigners" have to go to police headquarters, often very early in the morning, and wait outside in line for a police officer who would finally receive them, often in a not very dignified manner, to speak euphemistically.

In the years of globalization, some of the same mechanisms went on in a number of countries, but once again with different categories presiding over the creation of who is the outcast, from Colombia (Iturralde 2008) to Argentina (Brandariz García and Monclús Masó, 2015), from the Republic of South Africa (Kempa and Singh 2008; Vigneswaran 2013), which has become a real attraction for a lot of people migrating from Central Africa, to Israel, where 40 per cent of the working population is made up of "migrants" (Ajzenstadt and Shapira 2012). Even more so in the

Middle East and especially in the Gulf States, countries like Qatar,[3] Saudi Arabia, the United Arab Emirates. In some of these countries, as we have seen, the section of the population that is immigrants is 70 or 80 per cent; basically the native born are the upper class, everyone else is an immigrant, and many of them seem to be living in almost basic survival conditions. Most are people from East Asia, from the Philippines, Pakistan, Sri Lanka, Bangladesh; they live in camps that are not that far from barracks essentially, under temperatures of 50 degrees centigrade in the summer (Hari 2009). They have basically no rights to speak of. Other centres of this development are in Australia, Malaysia, Singapore and Hong Kong. Also in Australia, an intensification of a policing-attitude in relation to migration has developed together with an expansion of the "policing of the border" to include seas and ships (Weber 2012; Pickering and Weber 2013; Pickering 2014), very similar to what happened in the Mediterranean (Campesi 2011). In Hong Kong, Francesco Vecchio's (2014) description of the life of refugees and asylum seekers shows how the regulation of immigration and asylum, in countries that are catalysts for migration, by prescribing unrealistically narrow immigration thresholds or cumbersome and complicated entry procedures, ends up constructing a *de facto* regulation that by implication exposes those migrants who "make it in" to insecurity, marginalization and exploitation. At the same time, such processes are connected to instances of criminalization and racialization of those very migrants. These asylum seekers and irregular migrants come from a range of countries, including Africa, Pakistan, Bangladesh, etc. Given immigration norms in Hong Kong, they are not allowed to work while their cases are being considered (or not considered if undocumented), yet they need to work in order to live. They end up therefore finding themselves in a difficult situation, one that we know very well from similar conditions in Europe. Many wind up residing in highly "invisible" quarters, such as Chungking Mansions (Mathews 2007) and in rural areas of Hong Kong. Here they try to remain invisible but they really cannot because of their "non-Chinese" "look".

Also, Maggy Lee (2013, 2014), starting from a perspective rooted in China and more specifically in Hong Kong, analyses especially the phenomenon of human trafficking, a perspective that inserts itself into a burgeoning interest in the "gendering" of borders (Marmo and Smith 2012; Pickering et al. 2014). Whereas this has started to mean, recently, an interest in the intersection of migration controls

---

[3]See *The Guardian*'s exposure of the tens of thousands of "slave" migrants who are working on the preparations for the 2022 World Cup, amidst "exploitation and abuses that amount to modern-day slavery" with predictions of a total of "four thousand migrant workers dead" at the end of the building binge and general disregard for any sort of workers' rights (www.theguardian.com/world/2013/sep/25/revealed-qatars-world-cup-slaves/; accessed 10 February 2015).

and the construction of male gender (Kaufman 2013, 2014; Ugelvik 2014), the traditional concern with trafficking has focused upon a specific characterization of women migrants, mirroring the view of women in a patriarchal society. In such society women are seen as destined to the private control of men (within some concept of "the family") as opposed to the public control of the state – generally reserved to men or to specific categories of "deviant" women (usually perceived as "masculine" women) – what Segrave et al. (2009) describe as the dichotomy between the "infantilized" versus the "demonized" trafficked woman. This view, that goes back all the way to Lombroso (Lombroso and Ferrero 1893), was at the basis of the concern, as we have seen, for the trafficking of "white slave" women (Knepper 2014: 489–93) and the restriction of women's independent migration to the United States in the early decades of the twentieth century. It reappears in the "virginity testing" on non-Western migrant women at the British borders in the 1970s (Marmo and Smith 2012) as well as in contemporary practices and views about trafficking and border controls on women (Lee 2011, 2013, 2014; Pickering 2014).

In Japan too there is a "convergence" of control on immigration and crime (Yamamoto and Johnson 2014). One of the most interesting situations, however, is the situation in China, which has to do with *internal* and not *external* migrants. In fact, with the very sustained development pace of the last few decades, we have witnessed a sort of gigantic and time-compressed reproduction of what Marx had called "primitive" or "original" accumulation (of "variable" capital: labour) when hundreds of millions of people relocated themselves from the countryside to the cities. In China, this contemporary process has to do with the institution that the Chinese call *hukou*, the local population registry (and related regulation of residence), something created, or anyway strengthened, by Mao Zedong.[4] The premise of such regulation was that to live in cities is a privilege (Wang 2004; Wu and Treiman 2004; Chan and Buckingham 2008[5]), and that many people from the countryside wanted to go to live in the city and so only some people should have that privilege. The *hukou* regulation somehow made that possible. What happened with the huge development, the so-called Chinese miracle, in the last ten or fifteen years, was that between 200 and 300 million people moved from the countryside to the cities without being allowed to do so, basically without having the papers. People have been building whole new cities overnight in China and there was the need for, and the opportunity

---

[4]For a Taiwanese variation see Martin (2013).

[5]I thank Karen Joe and Valeria Ferraris for pointing out to me the literature in this section and more generally for the information on China.

to, work.[6] In fact, the internal migrant issue is often referred to as China's "floating population" because the worker moving from rural to urban areas finds himself or herself, for a range of reasons, including *hukou*, on an internal circuit – looking for new jobs and opportunities (Chan forthcoming). Construction finishes or comes to a halt, and they have to move on. With this circuit, men work in the "traditional" jobs and women also work in factories, construction sites and in the sex industry. Alongside issues of family separation, education for children, housing, etc., there has been a rise in crime and victimization among migrants themselves (Xu 2009). In fact, not to have the *hukou* permit means that one does not have the right of residence, cannot send children to school, is not part of the welfare system. In short, it means that one is not part of social life (we are talking about between 200 and 300 million people). This is so true that alternative arrangements have sprung up in the cities – facilities for school, welfare and health – essentially reserved for people without the right of residence (Friedman 2013).

The 2013 Third Plenum of the Chinese Communist Party introduced some changes, having to do especially with the betterment of the situation of peasants in the countryside and their property rights, and this eventually will have some effect also on the discipline of the *hukou*. The *hukou* is already now characterized by different rules according to the place and the social standing of the person or group to which it is applied. For instance, across the border from Hong Kong twenty years ago there was a little fishing village, called Shen Zhen, organized during the opening up period in the 1980s as one of China's special economic zones; it is now a city as large as New York, with about 15 million people. It went up in ten to fifteen years. Lisa Zhong (2009) studied "community policing" in this city. There are whole neighbourhoods of Shen Zhen where 70–80 per cent of the population are "illegal", people without a *hukou* permit, and these are the neighbourhoods with high prostitution, high crime, problems with security, where people are afraid to go. People from Hong Kong would cross there to have so-called "mercenary sex" and to buy drugs, but they are really afraid of going there. One of the top prosecutors of the city has denounced "the migrants" as "responsible for 80 per cent of crime".[7] We are not talking about "undocumented"

---

[6]See also the analysis by Mezzadra and Neilson (2013: 220–8). During the construction of skyscrapers, being built by the hundreds in China in the last twenty years or so, often the workers sleep in the skyscraper they are building, on the eleventh floor when they are working on the twelfth, and so on. The reason for that is a mix of "efficiency" by the employers, a money-saving device for the workers, but also a legal and not only economic difficulty with finding a place to sleep on the cheap.

[7]As reported in the *Nanfang Doushibao* (from *Internazionale* no. 932, page 29, 20 January 2012). See also Xu (2009).

foreign migrants in Southern Europe or any other of the places that we have just mentioned. This is "Communist" China. This is, especially, the process that has been feeding China's incredible development, especially in the construction industry.

So, from the place where migration law, criminal law and the economy intersect, there is a specific path to development, which is of course not given once and for all. It really depends on political struggle and political conflict; who has the power, who represents whom. In her 2005 work, Kitty Calavita had claimed the "structural" importance of the economy, by showing that Italy and Spain would basically follow the same policies even if each of them had been ruled at different times by governments with different political alignments, sometimes centre-left, sometimes centre-right. That may certainly be the case, but I would like to suggest that the other way around may also be true. It may very well be that given certain political conditions, emerging both within left-leaning and right-leaning majorities, have created an environment, a context, that has pushed toward what we could describe as a post-Fordist state of affairs, feeding on cheap and malleable labour (Young 2003, 2007). That may of course in turn be premised on more fundamental "structural" elements. Clearly, a strong, labour-intensive, high-productivity economy, such as Germany, may be less in need of cheap labour and more of skilled workers, whereas Italy, Spain or Greece may have tried to compete by importing labour cheaper than their own at the end of a rather intense period of labour conflict and class struggle.[8] Capitalism is an opportunistic set of arrangements. It adapts to situations at least as much as it contributes to and feeds back on them. In every country, the specific path taken may have been a combination of migration laws and ideas of citizenship steeped in culture and history, idiosyncratic images of social, national and "racial" groups, processes of criminalization, all connected with given economic strengths and weaknesses. It is the specific combination of elements in each historical circumstance that in the end drives development even if, abstractly, such elements may appear similar across all circumstances. Indeed, as we have seen, "all societies produce strangers; but each kind of society produces its own kind of strangers, and produces them in its own inimitable way" (Bauman 1995: 1).

One finds oneself therefore in a real quandary. Because, without exploitation of migratory movements by newly invested capital, we would not have this very investment – or perhaps we would have investment in technology, i.e. a constant or "fixed" type of capital, as happened recently in Germany. We would have no migration, however, and migration has traditionally been the trigger to deep social and cultural change. It is therefore hard to resist the conclusion that – as the old Marxian saying goes – "the only answer lies in class struggle." Because

---

[8]There is a whole "theory of the cycle" about this (Melossi 2008: 229–52, 2010c, 2013d).

today in China, for example, the preoccupation of political leadership with civil and industrial unrest is very real and has even given rise to rumours about a possible reconsideration of the whole *hukou* regulation system, which is appearing increasingly as a check on development that is no longer tolerable.[9] But the question is much more complex than that, because, like in Southern Europe with undocumented "external" migrants, the issue is not really one of impeding such developments but of making possible the creation of a pariah caste constructed legally ("legally" not as in "according to the law" but as in "by means of the law"), through the legal marginalization of migrants without documents, whether external or internal, and their exploitation as cheap "illegal" labour, an exploitation made possible by their very *legal* marginalization. Of course this is only possible while there are plenty of workers ready to cut each other's throats competing for work. Even in labour-rich China that time is coming to an end. With an overheated economy developing at a rate of 8–10 per cent of increase in per capita national product every year, labour shortages have started to appear and, together with them, strikes, demands for huge wage increases, grass-root organizing and all the other accoutrements of class conflict, including a new Labour Contract Law, introduced in 2008, that instead of diffusing the workers' demands has, as always in such cases, encouraged and emboldened them.[10] All of this will push wages and standards of living up, eventually equalizing the standards of the Chinese working class to those of their European and American competitors (in a way not dissimilar from what happened in Southern Europe between the 1960s and 1980s!). However, in order to have such deep, and welcome, social and cultural changes, one has to have capital's profitability to invest, which, in the infancy of the economic cycle, translates into those conditions of quasi-servile labour that we have reported in many other parts of the world.

As Angela Davis was warning us at the beginning of this section, "[m]ore prisons are being built to catch the lives disrupted by movements of capital, people who cannot find a place for themselves in this new society governed by capital end up going to prison". Prisons are then built "to catch those people who have been deprived of their land and have no source of cash". People have been deprived of their source of sustenance and have no source of cash. In a nutshell, here are the

---

[9]It is quite interesting that the reform of the *hukou* system was announced together with a plan to reduce or even eliminate the system of rehabilitation camps through forced labour (from the *South China Morning Post*, Hong Kong, as reported in *Internazionale* no. 982, page 11, 11 January 2013).

[10]See www.lexology.com/library/detail.aspx?g=737da783-b32d-4c70-b243-613d79032b02 (accessed 10 February 2015).

roots of the crime and here are the roots of the punishment. Their victimization is double in so far as they are "destined" to commit certain kinds of crimes – those that the police are inherently geared to find out about – and are "destined" to be punished for those crimes. Now, vagrancy and banditism are no longer only prerogatives of the West – as was already clear when Eric Hobsbawm (1959) was studying "social banditism" in the 1950s and 1960s – but have expanded to almost every corner of the globe where there are people who are deprived of their means of sustenance but "have no source of cash", i.e. have not (successfully) entered yet into the monetary economy. So, perhaps, the world-wide re-discovery of the prison institution that started in the 1980s, after a period when the prevalent talk was of "decarceration" and "obsolescence" (Scull 1977; Cohen 1985), has something to do with that institution again rediscovering its perennial "clients", when a now globalized prison opens its doors to a former peasant class that is again supposed to be processed in order to become working class. A prison institution that – never mind the level of technological social development, ideas on the ends of punishment, or sophisticated accounts of prison-as-warehouse or "new penologies" – is to impart to the new recruits the evergreen lessons of subordination, order and discipline, so that they too may become what we already are.

in conclusion: crime, migration, social change and innovation

The processes of criminalization of migrants depend therefore, to a large extent, on the receiving norms and practices of the countries where they are admitted. The issue of legal status in particular is paramount for processes of criminalization. A key element seems to be the possession, by recent immigrants, of legal documentation that enables them to work. Work is an essential element of integration, and usually the possession of legal documents is a prerequisite for work. So in European countries generally the process of criminalization is related not so much to the status of immigrant as to the status of "undocumented" immigrant. The tradition of the continental police state is quite important in this respect (Foucault 1976; Campesi 2009). As we have seen, in many parts of Europe, at least before the "great recession" that started in 2008, migrants and asylum seekers were coming undocumented or overstayed waiting for the (at least in the pre-crisis era) almost unavoidable provision that "regularized" them, whether collectively or individually. In between, a dangerous period of lack of documentation ensued, fraught with the necessity of all sorts of illegalities.

We have seen that the situation in the United States is instead quite different. In short, the easier the processes of legal integration in the host society (residency and naturalization), the lower the criminalization processes. Conversely, the harder the process of legal inclusion, the higher the numbers of criminalized foreigners. Already in 1999, in a pioneering comparative study, James Lynch and Rita Simon had pointed out that "immigrant nations", such as the United States, Canada and Australia, have relatively open immigrant policies and high proportions of foreign-born within the resident population. Germany and Japan ("non-traditional immigrant nations") have restrictive immigration policies, strict policies for the control of resident aliens and restrictive naturalization policies. France and England have restrictive admission policies based on race and national origin, but naturalization policies are relatively open. Comparing the incarceration rates, the pattern that emerges across the seven nations is that, overall, immigrants in traditional immigrant-receiving countries have lower criminalization rates than non-traditional immigrant nations. The apparent relationship between the inclusiveness of immigration policies and the criminal involvement of aliens suggests that the more restrictive the policy, the greater the criminalization of foreigners.

So, in a sense we can say that basic features of society generate the policies of reception toward the various groups. There may be, of course, various economic periods and economic needs. What I think emerged from this all too brief review, however, was that there are different cultural attitudes toward "migrants", "strangers" and specific groups of minorities that may or may not overlap with migrants. These attitudes tend to drive, by and large, the policies of reception and create the environment inside which phenomena of crime and punishment – that, as we know from the core of criminological reflection, can never really be separated in so far as one constitutes the other – do somehow relate to the issue of migration. So, in societies where the migrant status is essentially considered in a benign way, and where it is connected to a "democratic" view that promotes social change and social innovation – change and innovation of which migrants are in a sense the torchbearers – such as in the United States, the rates of criminalization of migrants are lower. Here there is, however, at the same time a long history of racism, rooted in the question of slavery and in deep forms of racial prejudice at the time of the nineteenth century. Then, the societal attitude toward migrants does not transform itself into processes of criminalization until the migrants' second generations, when the children of migrants settle in social areas marred by marginalization, poverty and forms of ghettoization. These forms of ghettoization, however, are much harsher for children of migrants who are perceived as belonging in certain ethnic groups. Criminalization reflects these social conditions because these are at the same time at the roots of differential participation in criminal behaviour and differential exposure to the risks of criminalization – first of all through the work of police and secondarily of the other formal control apparatuses (courts and prisons essentially).

This is the case for the United States and, to a minor extent, for the other countries that constituted themselves as countries based on immigration. Very different is the case of European countries – even if there are some European countries, such as the UK, France and the Netherlands, where immigration flows were initially connected to their colonial status, where immigration has been going on for quite some time, and where the attitude toward immigration is somewhat less benign than in true immigrants' countries but more benign than in countries that have never experienced immigration. The latter are most of the other countries that we have mentioned, from Southern Europe to the Middle East to Asia. These are countries that are generally speaking culturally and socially more conservative, with an established social stratification whereby the destiny of migrants is ineluctably to be integrated at the bottom. This basic attitude is reflected in the difficulty in immigrating legally, and in the somewhat hostile attitude toward innovation and therefore also toward phenomena of deviance. These countries experience therefore the marginalization of first generation migrants, given that the need for migrants is there and migrants manage to come or stay anyway even if illegally (but, differently from the US situation, it is much harder for them to "pass" as legal).

A special case is the European Union, which, as we have seen, should really be considered as a political entity separated from the various national European countries and also different from that peculiar historical and cultural reality that is understood in the concept of "Europe". As such, the EU has been increasingly trying – in this as in other policy areas – to play an important role of homogenization and harmonization among the various national policies, given that a common immigration policy is a requirement of the construction of the EU as a cohesive economic, political and social reality. Here the role of Germany is essential, not only because it is the most important immigration area in the EU but also because it is increasingly the power core of the EU. In Germany, as we have seen, already in 1998 the new red–green government proclaimed aloud that *Deutschland ist ein Einwanderungsland!* ("Germany is an immigration land!") (Monte 2002). Now we need to proclaim aloud that "the EU is an immigration land!" and as such it has to equip itself not only with the norms but also with the institutions and the tools that would allow the EU to actually play the role of an immigration land, to become a true country of immigrants, which is *de facto* what already it is now. This is by no means the least of the policy areas where the credibility and the reality of the existence of a EU will play out in the next few years. As we have seen, however, this is strictly intertwined with the creation and the struggle for a different European "public sphere" – as Jürgen Habermas would call it – one where, increasingly, social innovation (and therefore internal mobility and mobility from the outside) are welcome. This process is inextricably linked with the construction of a common cultural area and, increasingly in the future, also a common linguistic area. It is indeed impossible to separate – I have argued for this elsewhere at greater length (Melossi 2005) – the three aspects: the construction of the EU and its cultural and linguistic harmonization, the establishment of a cultural area characterized by the hegemony of social change and innovation, and an autonomous and increasingly European policy about immigration. The easing of the legal status of migrants – and the establishment of a different channel to European citizenship for third parties autonomous from the citizenship of the constituent member states – will be the necessary premise for an easing also of processes of migrants' criminalization. The migrants' participation in criminal enterprises will in fact reduce and, together with it, also the pressure of formal social control on migrants. In a situation in which, hopefully, the European Union is slowly, unevenly and, even if somewhat licking its wounds, walking toward economic recovery, a more rational, better planned and more receptive policy toward immigrants is an absolute priority because, together with economic recovery, the pressure on European borders will start again and we must be ready to welcome migrants.

We have seen that countries historically based in immigration show less crime by immigrants and less punishment of immigrants. It is therefore a pity – and it looks like very poor political wisdom – that some of them now want to shy away from a tradition, and a promise, of which they should be proud. Were such changes to be put in effect, they would probably reach an opposite result to the one for which they were ostensibly intended. This is also an excellent illustration of the enduring value of the approach, in the sociology of deviance and crime, which, in the 1960s, was dubbed the "labelling approach". The experience of Europe and of the United States (in spite of the efforts by conservative Americans to follow, as usual, the worst European examples instead of being true to the best American tradition) teaches us that if we want to decrease the participation and involvement of migrants in criminal activities we have to do exactly the opposite of what we have been told for years, i.e. we have to welcome migrants in our midst. This will also be the best policy in order to prevent migrants' crime as well as migrants' criminalization.

references

AAS, Katja Franko (2007) "Analysing a World in Motion: Global Flows Meet 'Criminology of the Other'." *Theoretical Criminology* 11: 283–303.

AAS, Katja Franko (2011) "'Crimmigrant' Bodies and Bona Fide Travelers: Surveillance, Citizenship and Global Governance." *Theoretical Criminology* 15: 331–46.

AAS, Katja Franko (2013) "The Ordered and the Bordered Society: Migration Control, Citizenship, and the Northern Penal State," in K. F. Aas and M. Bosworth (eds), *The Borders of Punishment: Migration, Citizenship, and Social Exclusion*. Oxford: Oxford University Press. pp. 21–39.

AAS, Katja Franko and Mary Bosworth (2013) (eds) *The Borders of Punishment: Migration, Citizenship, and Social Exclusion*. Oxford: Oxford University Press.

ADDAMS, Jane (1910 [1998]) *Twenty Years at Hull-House*. New York: Penguin Books.

AGAMBEN, Giorgio (1995 [1998]) *Homo Sacer: Sovereign Power and Bare Life*. Stanford: Stanford University Press.

AGOZINO, Biko (2003) *Counter-Colonial Criminology: A Critique of Imperialist Reason*. London: Pluto Press.

AJZENSTADT, Mimi and Assaf Shapira (2012) "The Socio-Legal Construction of Otherness under a Neo-Liberal Regime: The Case of Foreign Workers in the Israeli Criminal Courts." *British Journal of Criminology* 52: 685–704.

ALBRECHT, Hans-Jörg (1997) "Ethnic Minorities, Crime, and Criminal Justice in Germany," in Michael Tonry (ed.), *Ethnicity, Crime, and Immigration: Comparative and Cross-National Perspectives*. Chicago: University of Chicago Press. pp. 31–99.

ALEXANDER, Michelle (2012) *The New Jim Crow: Mass Incarceration in the Age of Colorblindness*. New York: The New Press.

ALIVERTI, Ana (2012) "Making People Criminal: The Role of the Criminal Law in Immigration Enforcement." *Theoretical Criminology* 16: 417–34.

ALIVERTI, Ana (2013) *Crimes of Mobility: Criminal Law and the Regulation of Immigration*. London: Routledge.

AMBROSINI, Maurizio (2009) "L'ennesima ultima sanatoria." Available at: www.lavoce. info (accessed 1 September 2009).

AMNESTY INTERNATIONAL (2008) "Jailed without Justice: Immigration Detention in the USA." Report.

ANDERSON, Elijah (1990) *Streetwise. Race, Class and Change in an Urban Community*. Chicago: The University of Chicago Press.

ANDERSON, Nels (1923 [1967]) *The Hobo*. Chicago: University of Chicago Press.

ANDERSON, Nels (1940 [1974]) *Men on the Move*. Chicago: University of Chicago Press.

ARCHER, Dane and Rosemary Gartner (1984) *Violence and Crime in Cross-National Perspective*. New Haven, CT: Yale University Press.

ARRIGHI, Giovanni (1994) *The Long Twentieth Century: Money, Power, and the Origins of Our Times*. London: Verso.

ASBURY, Herbert (1928 [2008]) *The Gangs of New York: An Informal History of the Underworld*. New York: Knopf Doubleday Publishing Group.

BARAN, Paul A. and Paul M. Sweezy (1966) *Monopoly Capital: An Essay on American Economy and Social Order*. New York: Monthly Review Press.

BARBAGLI, Marzio (2008) *Immigrazione e sicurezza in Italia*. Bologna: il Mulino.

BARKER, Vanessa (2013) "Policing Membership in Husby: Four Factors to the Stockholm Riots." Post for Borders of Criminologies Research Network (31 May 2013).

BAUMAN, Zygmunt (1995) "Making and Unmaking of Strangers." *Thesis Eleven*, November, 43: 1–16.

BAUMAN, Zygmunt (1997) *Postmodernity and Its Discontents*. Cambridge: Polity Press.

BECK, Ulrich (1997 [2000]) *What Is Globalization?* Cambridge: Polity Press.

BECKETT, Katherine and Steve Herbert (2010) *Banished: The New Social Control in Urban America*. New York: Oxford University Press.

BELL, Daniel (1953) "Crime as an American Way of Life." *The Antioch Review* 13: 131–54 (included in D. Bell 1960 [2000] *The End of Ideology: On the Exhaustion of Political Ideas in the Fifties*. Cambridge, MA: Havard University Press).

BERARDI, Luca and Sandra M. Bucerius (2014) "Immigrants and Their Children: Evidence on Generational Differences in Crime," in S. M. Bucerius and M. Tonry (eds), *Ethnicity, Crime, and Immigration*. New York: Oxford University Press. pp. 551–83.

BERMAN, Marshall (1982 [1988]) *All That Is Solid Melts Into Air*. New York: Penguin Books.

BITTNER, Egon (1967) "The Police on Skid-Row: A Study of Peace Keeping." *American Sociological Review* 32: 699–715.

BODY-GENDROT, Sophie (2014) "Ethnicity, Crime, and Immigration in France," in S. M. Bucerius and M. Tonry (eds), *Ethnicity, Crime, and Immigration*. New York: Oxford University Press. pp. 708–37.

BODY-GENDROT, Sophie and Catherine Wihtold de Wenden (2003) *Police et discriminations raciales, le tabou français*. Paris: Ed. de l'atelier.

BOSWORTH, Mary and M. Guild (2008) "Governing Through Migration Control." *British Journal of Criminology* 48: 703–19.

BOWERS, William J. and Glenn L. Pierce (1980) "Deterrence or Brutalization: What Is the Effect of Executions?" *Crime and Delinquency* 26: 453–84.

BOX, Stephen and Chris Hale (1982) "Economic Crisis and the Rising Prisoner Population." *Crime and Social Justice* 17: 20–35.

BRANDARIZ GARCÍA, José Ángel and Marta Monclús Masó (2015) *Políticas y prácticas de control de fronteras: Estudio comparativo del control de los migrantes en el contexto latinoamericano y europeo*. Buenos Aires: Didot.

BROTHERTON, David C. (2008a) "Youth Subcultures, Resistance, and the Street Organization in Late Modern New York," in Michael Flynn and David C. Brotherton (eds), *Globalizing the Streets: Cross-Cultural Perspectives on Youth, Control and Empowerment*. New York: Columbia University Press.

BROTHERTON, David C. (2008b) "Beyond Social Reproduction: Bringing Resistance Back in Gang Theory." *Theoretical Criminology* 12: 55–77.

BUCERIUS, Sandra M. and Michael Tonry (eds) (2014) *Ethnicity, Crime, and Immigration*. New York: Oxford University Press.

BULMER, Martin (1984) *The Chicago School of Sociology*. Chicago: University of Chicago Press.

BURROUGH, Bryan (2005) *Public Enemies: America's Greatest Crime Wave and the Birth of the FBI, 1933–34.* New York: Penguin Books.

BURSIK, Robert (2006) "Rethinking the Chicago School of Criminology: A New Era of Immigration," in R. Martinez Jr and A. Valenzuela (eds), *Immigration and Crime: Race, Ethnicity and Violence.* New York: New York University Press. pp. 20–35.

BUTCHER, Kristin F. and Anne Morrison Piehl (2007) "Why Are Immigrants' Incarceration Rates so Low? Evidence on Selective Immigration, Deterrence, and Deportation." Working Paper 13229, National Bureau of Economic Research.

CALAVITA, Kitty (2005) *Immigrants at the Margins: Law, Race, and Exclusion in Southern Europe.* New York: Cambridge University Press.

CAMPESI, Giuseppe (2009) *Genealogia della pubblica sicurezza. Teoria e storia del moderno dispositivo poliziesco.* Verona: Ombre Corte.

CAMPESI, Giuseppe (2011) "The Arab Spring and the Crisis of the European Border Regime: Manufacturing Emergency in the Lampedusa Crisis." *EUI Working Papers,* RSCAS 2011/59. http://cadmus.eui.eu/handle/1814/19375.

CAMPESI, Giuseppe (2013) *La detenzione amministrativa degli stranieri.* Rome: Carocci.

CAMPESI, Giuseppe (2015) "Hindering the deportation machine. An ethnography of power and resistance in immigration detention," *Punishment and Society.*

CAPPETTI, Carla (1993) *Writing Chicago.* New York: Columbia University Press.

CARITAS/Migrantes (2009) "La criminalità degli immigrati: dati, interpretazioni, pregiudizi," in *Guida per l'informazione sociale. Edizione 2010.* Capodarco di Fermo: Redattore Sociale. pp. 580–603.

CARITAS/Migrantes (2010) *Immigrazione. Dossier statistico 2010.* Rome: Idos.

CASTELLS, Manuel (1996) *The Rise of the Network Society.* Oxford: Blackwell.

CASTLES, Stephen and Mark J. Miller (2009) *The Age of Migration: International Population Movements in the Modern World,* 5th edn. Basingstoke: Palgrave Macmillan.

CAVALLI-SFORZA, Luigi Luca and Daniela Padoan (2013) *Razzismo e noismo.* Turin: Einaudi.

CEOBANU, Alin M. (2011) "Usual Suspects? Public Views about Immigrants' Impact on Crime in European Countries." *International Journal of Comparative Sociology* 52 (1–2): 114–31.

CHAMBLISS, William (1964) "A Sociological Analysis of the Law of Vagrancy." *Social Problems* 12: 45–69.

CHAMBLISS, William J. (1973) "The Roughnecks and the Saints." *Society* November/December: 24–31.

CHAMBLISS, William (1978) *On the Take: From Petty Crooks to Presidents.* Bloomington: Indiana University Press.

CHAN, Kam Wing (forthcoming) "China, Internal Migration," in Immanuel Ness and Peter Bellwood (eds), *The Encyclopedia of Global Migration.* Oxford: Blackwell.

CHAN, Kam Wing and Will Buckingham (2008) "Is China Abolishing the Hukou System?" *The China Quarterly* 195: 582–606.

CHELIOTIS, Leonidas K. (ed.) (2013) "Special Section: Immigration Detention around Europe." *European Journal of Criminology* 10: 690–759.

CHEVALIER, Louis (1958 [2000]) *Labouring Classes and Dangerous Classes: In Paris during the First Half of the Nineteenth Century.* New York: Howard Fertig.

CHRISTIE, Nils (1986) "Suitable Enemies," in H. Bianchi and R. Van Swaaningen (eds), *Abolitionism.* Amsterdam: Free University Press. pp. 42–54.

CLOWARD, Richard and Lloyd Ohlin (1960) *Delinquency and Opportunity: A Theory of Delinquent Gangs.* Glencoe, IL: Free Press.

COHEN, Stanley (1985) *Visions of Social Control*. Cambridge: Polity Press.

CRESSEY, Donald R. (1968) "Culture Conflict, Differential Association, and Normative Conflict," in M. E. Wolfgang (ed.), *Crime and Culture: Essays in Honor of Thorsten Sellin*. New York: Wiley. pp. 43–54.

CROCITTI, Stefania (2011) "I minori stranieri e italiani tra scuola, lavoro e devianza: un'indagine di self-report." *Studi Sulla Questione Criminale* 6 (1): 65–106.

CROCITTI, Stefania (2014) "Immigration, Crime, and Criminalization in Italy," in S. M. Bucerius and M. Tonry (eds), *Ethnicity, Crime, and Immigration*. New York: Oxford University Press. pp. 791–833.

DAHRENDORF, Ralf (1985) *Law and Order*. London: Stevens.

DAUVERGNE, Catherine (2008) *Making People Illegal: What Globalization Means for Migration and Law*. Cambridge: Cambridge University Press.

DAVIES, Garth and Jeffrey Fagan (2012) "Crime and Enforcement in Immigrant Neighborhoods: Evidence from New York City." *Annals of the American Academy of Political and Social Science* 641: 99–124.

DAVIS, Angela (2003) *Are Prisons Obsolete?* New York: Seven Stories Press.

DAVIS, Angela (2014) "Interview with …" *Social Justice* 40 (1–2): 37–53.

DAVIS, Mike (1990) *City of Quartz: Excavating the Future in Los Angeles*. London: Verso.

DE GENOVA, Nicholas P. (2002) "Migrant 'Illegality' and Deportability in Everyday Life." *Annual Review of Anthropology* 31: 419–47.

DE GIORGI, Alessandro (2002 [2006]) *Re-thinking the Political Economy of Punishment: Perspectives on Post-fordism and Penal Politics*. Aldershot and Burlington, VT: Ashgate.

DEEGAN, Mary Jo (1988) *Jane Addams and the Men of the Chicago School, 1892–1918*. New Brunswick, NJ: Transaction Books.

DIAMANTI, Ilvo (ed.) (2012) *L'insicurezza sociale ed economica in Italia e in Europa: Significati, immagine e realtà*. Yearly Report. Fondazione Unipolis, Bologna and Osservatorio di Pavia, Pavia.

DOUGLAS, Mary (1966 [2003]) *Purity and Danger: An Analysis of Concepts of Pollution and Taboo*. London: Routledge.

DREISER, Theodore (1900 [1981]) *Sister Carrie*. New York: Penguin Group.

DUBOIS, William E. B. (1899 [1996]) *The Philadelphia Negro: A Social Study*. Philadelphia: University of Pennsylvania Press.

DUMM, Thomas L. (1987) *Democracy and Punishment: Disciplinary Origins of the United States*. Madison: University of Wisconsin Press.

DUNCAN, Martha G. (1996) *Romantic Outlaws, Beloved Prisons*. New York: New York University Press.

DURKHEIM, Emile (1893 [1963]) *The Division of Labour in Society*. New York: Free Press.

DURKHEIM, Emile (1895 [1938]) *The Rules of Sociological Method*. New York: Free Press.

ENGBERSEN, Godfried, Arjen Leerkes and Erik Snel (2014) "Ethnicity, Migration, and Crime in the Netherlands," in S. M. Bucerius and M. Tonry (eds), *Ethnicity, Crime, and Immigration*. New York: Oxford University Press. pp. 766–90.

ENGEL, Robin S. and Kristin Swartz (2014) "Race, Crime, and Policing," in S. M. Bucerius and M. Tonry (eds), *Ethnicity, Crime, and Immigration*. New York: Oxford University Press. pp.135–65.

ENGELS, Friederich (1845 [1975]) *The Condition of the Working Class in England in 1844*. New York: International.

ERIKSON, Kai (1966) *Wayward Puritans*. New York: John Wiley.

EUROPEAN COMMISSION (2009) *Report from the Commission to the European Parliament and the Council: First Annual Report on Immigration and Asylum.*

FABINI, Giulia (2014) "The Illegal Immigration Law: A Regime of Law, Discourses, and Police Practices." *AmeriQuest Online Journal* 11(2).

FABINI, Giulia (forthcoming) "The Factory of Suitable Enemies. Acceptable Levels of Illegality at the Italian Internal Border." Doctoral dissertation. "Renato Treves" PhD Programme in Law and Society, University of Milan.

FARRIS, Robert E. L. and H. Warren Dunham (1934) *Mental Disorders in Urban Areas.* Chicago: University of Chicago Press.

FEDERN, Paul (1919–20) "Zür Psychologie der Revolution: die vaterlose Gesellschaft." *Der Oesterreichische Volkswirt* 11: 571–4, 595–8.

FERRACUTI, Franco (1968) "European Migration and Crime," in M. E. Wolfgang (ed.), *Crime and Culture: Essays in Honor of Thorsten Sellin.* New York: Wiley. pp. 189–219.

FERRARIS, Valeria (2009) "Migrants' Offside Trap: A Strategy for Dealing with Misleading Rules and a Hostile Playing Field," in J. Shapland and P. Ponsaers (eds), *The Informal Economy and Connections with Organized Crime: The Impact of National Social and Economic Policies.* The Hague: Boom Legal Publishers.

FERRI, Enrico (1884a [1979]) *Sociologia criminale.* Milan: Feltrinelli.

FERRI, Enrico (1884b [2009]) "The Data of Criminal Statistics, continued," in Nicole Rafter (ed.), *The Origins of Criminology: A Reader.* Abingdon: Routledge. pp. 330–6.

FITZGERALD, Marian (1995) "'Race' and Crime: The facts?" Paper presented at the British Society of Criminology, Loughborough, July.

FOUCAULT, Michel (1975 [1977]) *Discipline and Punish.* New York: Pantheon.

FOUCAULT, Michel (1976 [2003]) *Society Must Be Defended.* New York: Picador.

FRIEDMAN, Eli (2013) "Outside the New China," *Jacobin Magazine* 11–12.

GARLAND, David (2001) *The Culture of Control: Crime and Social Order in Contemporary Society.* Oxford: Oxford University Press.

GIBNEY, Matthew J. (2013) "Deportation, Crime, and the Changing Character of Membership in the United Kingdom," in Katja Franko Aas and Mary Bosworth (eds), *The Borders of Punishment: Migration, Citizenship, and Social Exclusion.* Oxford: Oxford University Press. pp. 218–36.

GIDDENS, Anthony (1984) *The Constitution of Society.* Berkeley: University of California Press.

GILROY, Paul (1987) *There Ain't No Black in the Union Jack.* London: Hutchinson/Unwin.

GILROY, Paul (1993) *The Black Atlantic: Modernity and Double Consciousness.* Cambridge, MA: Harvard University Press, London and New York: Verso.

GLOWACKI, Peggy and Julia Hendry (2004) *Images of America: Hull-House.* Charleston, SC: Arcadia.

GOFFMAN, Alice (2014) *On the Run. Fugitive Life in an American City.* Chicago: University of Chicago Press.

GOFFMAN, Erving (1963) *Stigma.* Englewood Cliffs, NJ: Prentice-Hall.

GONZALES, Roberto G. (2011) "Learning to Be Illegal: Undocumented Youth and Shifting Legal Contexts in the Transition to Adulthood." *American Sociological Review* 76: 602–19.

GONZALEZ, Juan (1999) *Harvest of Empire. A History of Latinos in America.* New York: Viking.

GORN, Elliot J. (2009) *Dillinger's Wild Ride: The Year That Made America's Public Enemy Number One.* Oxford: Oxford University Press.

GRAEBER, David (2011) *Debt. The first 5,000 years.* Brooklyn: Melville House.

GRAHAM, John and Benjamin Bowling (1995) *Young People and Crime.* London: Home Office Research Study 145.

GRAMSCI, Antonio (1929–1935 [1991–2007]) *Prison Notebooks,* 3 volumes. New York: Columbia University Press.

GREENBERG, David F. (1977) "The Dynamics of Oscillatory Punishment Processes." *Journal of Criminal Law and Criminology* 68: 643–51.

GUERINO, Paul, Paige M. Harrison and William J. Sabol (2011) *Prisoners in 2010.* Bulletin of December 2011, Bureau of Justice Statistics, Office of Justice Programs (Washington DC, US Department of Justice).

GUSFIELD, Joseph R. (1963) *Symbolic Crusade. Status Politics and the American Temperance Movement.* Urbana, IL: University of Illinois Press.

HAGAN, John and Alberto Palloni (1999) "Sociological Criminology and the Mythology of Hispanic Immigration and Crime." *Social Problems* 46: 617–32.

HAGAN, John, Ron Levi and Ronit Dinovitzer (2008) "The Symbolic Violence of the Crime–Immigration Nexus: Migrant Mythologies in the Americas." *Criminology & Public Policy* 7: 95–112.

HALL, Stuart, Chas Critcher, Tony Jefferson, John Clarke and Brian Roberts (1978) *Policing the Crisis: Mugging, the State, and Law and Order.* London: Macmillan.

HAMMAR, Tomas (1990) *Democracy and the Nation State: Aliens, Denizens, and Citizens in a World of International Migration.* Aldershot: Avebury.

HARCOURT, Bernard E. (2007) *Against Prediction: Profiling, Policing, and Punishing in an Actuarial Age.* Chicago: University of Chicago Press.

HARI, Johann (2009) "The Dark Side of Dubai." *The Independent,* 7 April 2009.

HAWKINS, Darnell F. (1995) *Ethnicity, Race, and Crime.* Albany: SUNY Press.

HIRSCHI, Travis (1969) *Causes of Delinquency.* Berkeley: University of California Press.

HIRSCHMAN, Albert O. (1977) *The Passions and the Interests.* Princeton: Princeton University Press.

HOBSBAWM, Eric J. (1959) *Primitive Rebels.* New York: The Norton Library.

HOCHSCHILD, Jennifer L. and Colin M. Brown (2014) "Searching (with Minimal Success) for Links between Immigration and Imprisonment," in S. M. Bucerius and M. Tonry (eds), *Ethnicity, Crime, and Immigration.* New York: Oxford University Press. pp. 663–707.

HOEFER, Michael, Nancy Rytina and Bryan C. Baker (2007) *Estimates of the Unauthorized Immigrant Population Residing in the United States: January 2007.* US Department of Homeland Security, Office of Immigration Statistics, Policy Directorate, available at: www.dhs.gov/xlibrary/assets/statistics/publications/ois_ill_pe_2007.pdf.

HORKHEIMER, Max and Theodor W. Adorno (1944 [1989]) *Dialectic of Enlightenment.* New York: Continuum.

HUDSON, Barbara (2008) "Difference, Diversity and Criminology: The Cosmopolitan Vision." *Theoretical Criminology* 12: 275–92.

IMBENI, Renzo (1993) "Report on EU's Citizenship," 21 December 1993, Commission of the European Parliament for Civil Liberties, Justice and Internal Affairs, A3-0437/93.

IMMIGRATION COMMISSION of the United States (1911) Report on "Immigration and Crime". 61th Cong., 3d Session, Senate Document 750, Volume 36.

INTERNATIONAL ORGANIZATION FOR MIGRATION (IOM) (2010) *Migration and the Economic Crisis in the European Union: Implications for Policy.* By Jobst Koehler, Frank Laczko, Christine Aghazarm, Julia Schad (Research and Publications Division). Brussels: International Organization for Migration.

ITURRALDE, Manuel (2008) "Emergency Penality and Authoritarian Liberalism: Recent Trends in Colombian Criminal Policy." *Theoretical Criminology* 12: 377–97.

JACOBS, James B. (1978) *Stateville: The Penitentiary in Mass Society*. Chicago: University of Chicago Press.

JAMES, William (1907 [1974]) *Pragmatism*. New York: The New American Library.

JANKOVIC, Ivan (1977) "Labor Market and Imprisonment." *Crime and Social Justice* 8: 17–31.

JENCKS, Christopher (1983) "Discrimination and Thomas Sowell." *The New York Review of Books* 3 March.

JOBARD, Fabien and René Lévy (2009) *Police et minorités visibles: les contrôles d'identité à Paris*. New York: Open Society Institute.

JOHANSEN, Nicolay B. (2013) "Governing the Funnel of Expulsion: Agamben, the Dynamics of Force, and Minimalist Biopolitics," in Katja Franko Aas and Mary Bosworth (eds), *The Borders of Punishment: Migration, Citizenship, and Social Exclusion*. Oxford: Oxford University Press. pp. 257–72.

JUNGER, Marianne (1989) "Discrepancies between Police and Self-Report Data for Dutch Racial Minorities." *British Journal of Criminology* 29: 273–84.

JUNGER-TAS, Josine (1997) "Ethnic Minorities and Criminal Justice in the Netherlands," in S. M. Bucerius and M. Tonry (eds), *Ethnicity, Crime, and Immigration*. New York: Oxford University Press. pp. 257–310.

JUNGER-TAS, Josine, I. H. Marshall, D. Enzmann, M. Killias, M. Steketee and B. Grusczynska (2010) *Juvenile Delinquency in Europe and Beyond: Results of the Second International Self-Report Delinquency Study*. Berlin/New York: Springer.

JUNGER-TAS, Josine, I. H. Marshall, D. Enzmann, M. Killias, M. Steketee and B. Grusczynska (2011) *The Many Faces of Youth Crime*. New York: Springer.

KAISER, Günther (1974) "Gastarbeiterkriminalität und ihre Erklärung als Kulturkonflikt," in T. Ansay and V. Gessner (eds), *Gastarbeiter in Gesellschaft und Recht*. Munich: Beck.

KANSTROOM, Daniel (2007) *Deportation Nation: Outsiders in American History*. Cambridge, MA: Harvard University Press.

KANSTROOM, Daniel (2012) *Aftermath: Deportation Law and the New American Diaspora*. Oxford: Oxford University Press.

KARMEN, Andrew (2000) *New York Murder Mystery: The True Story Behind the Crime Crash of the 1990s*. New York: New York University Press.

KAUFMAN, Emma (2013) "Hubs and Spokes: The Transformation of the British Prison," in Katja Franko Aas and Mary Bosworth (eds), *The Borders of Punishment: Migration, Citizenship, and Social Exclusion*. Oxford: Oxford University Press. pp. 166–82.

KAUFMAN, Emma (2014) "Gender at the Border: Nationalism and the New Logic of Punishment." *Punishment and Society* 16: 135–51.

KAZAN, Elia (1963) *America America* (film, USA).

KEMPA, Michael and Anne-Marie Singh (2008) "Private Security, Political Economy and the Policing of Race: Probing Global Hypotheses through the Case of South Africa." *Theoretical Criminology* 12: 333–54.

KIL, Sang Hea and Cecilia Menjívar (2006) "The 'War on the Border': Criminalizing Immigrants and Militarizing the U.S.–Mexico Border," in R. Martinez Jr and A. Valenzuela (eds), *Immigration and Crime: Race, Ethnicity and Violence*. New York: New York University Press. pp. 164–88.

KIL, Sang H., Cecilia Menjívar and Roxanne L. Doty (2009) "Securing Borders: Patriotism, Vigilantism and the Brutalization of the US American Public," in William F. McDonald (ed.), *Immigration, Crime and Justice*. Bingley: Emerald Group Publishing Limited. pp. 297–312.

KILLIAS, Martin (2011) *Immigration and Crime: The European Experience*. Research Report. San Domenico di Fiesole: European University Institute.

KING, Ryan D., Michael Massoglia and Christopher Uggen (2012) "Employment and Exile: U.S. Criminal Deportations, 1908–2005." *American Journal of Sociology* 117: 1786–825.

KIRK, David S., Andrew V. Papachristos, Jeffrey Fagan and Tom R. Tyler (2011) "The Paradox of Law Enforcement in Immigrant Communities: Does Tough Immigration Enforcement Undermine Public Safety?" *Annals of the American Academy of Political and Social Science* 641: 1–20.

KNEPPER, Paul (2014) "Traffickers? Terrorists? Smugglers? Immigrants in the United States and International Crime before World War II," in S. M. Bucerius and M. Tonry (eds), *Ethnicity, Crime, and Immigration*. New York: Oxford University Press. pp. 484–504.

KNIGHT, Louise W. (2005) *Citizen: Jane Addams and the Struggle for Democracy*. Chicago: University of Chicago Press.

KRASMANN, Susanne (2007) "The Enemy on the Border: Critique of a Programme in Favour of a Preventive State." *Punishment and Society* 9: 301–18.

LACEY, Nicola (2008) *The Prisoners' Dilemma: Political Economy and Punishment in Contemporary Democracies*. Cambridge: Cambridge University Press.

LAGRANGE, Hugues and Marco Oberti (eds) (2006) *Emeutes urbaines et protestations: une singularité française*. Paris: Presses de Sciences Po.

LEA, John and Jock Young (1984) *What Is to Be Done About Law and Order?* Harmondsworth: Penguin Books.

LEE, Maggy (2011) *Trafficking and Global Crime Control*. London: Sage.

LEE, Maggy (2013) "Human Trafficking and Border Control in the Global South," in Katja Franko Aas and Mary Bosworth (eds), *The Borders of Punishment: Migration, Citizenship, and Social Exclusion*. Oxford: Oxford University Press. pp. 128–45.

LEE, Maggy (2014) "Gendered Discipline and Protective Custody of Trafficking Victims in Asia." *Punishment and Society* 16: 206–22.

LEE, Matthew T. and Ramiro Martinez (2009) "Immigration Reduces Crime: An Emerging Scholarly Consensus," in William F. McDonald (ed.) *Immigration, Crime and Justice*. Bingley: Emerald Group Publishing Limited. pp. 3–16.

LEERKES, Arjen, Godfried Engbersen and Joanne van der Leun (2012) "Crime Among Irregular Immigrants and the Influence of Internal Border Control." *Crime Law and Social Change*, 58: 15–38.

LEMERT, Edwin M. (1951) *Social Pathology: A Systematic Approach to the Theory of Sociopathic Behavior*. New York: McGraw–Hill.

LÉVY, René and Hartwig Zander (1994) "Introduction," in G. Rusche and O. Kirchheimer (eds), *Peine et structure sociale*. Paris: Les Editions du Cerf. pp. 9–82.

LINDNER, Rolf (1990) *The Reportage of Urban Culture: Robert Park and the Chicago School*. Cambridge: Cambridge University Press.

LOMBROSO, Cesare (1896–7 [2006]) *Criminal Man* (translated with a new introduction by Mary Gibson and Nicole Hahn Rafter). Durham, NC: Duke University Press.

LOMBROSO, Cesare and Guglielmo Ferrero (1893 [2004]) *Criminal Woman, the Prostitute, and the Normal Woman* (translated with a new introduction by Mary Gibson and Nicole Hahn Rafter). Durham, NC: Duke University Press.

LOMBROSO, Cesare and Rodolfo Laschi (1890) *Il delitto politico e le rivoluzioni in rapporto al diritto, all'antropologia criminale ed alla scienza di governo*. Turin: Bocca.

LYNCH, James P. and Rita J. Simon (1999) "A Comparative Assessment of Criminal Involvement Among Immigrants and Natives Across Seven Nations." *International Criminal Justice Review* 9: 1–17.

MACDONALD, Arthur (1911) "Assassins of Rulers." *Journal of the American Institute of Criminal Law and Criminology* 2: 505–20.

MARMO, Marinella and Evan Smith (2012) "Female Migrants: Sex, Value and Credibility in Immigration Control," in J. McCulloch and S. Pickering (eds), *Borders and Crime: Pre-Crime, Mobility and Serious Harm in an Age of Globalization.* Houndmills, Basingstoke: Palgrave Macmillan. pp. 54–71.

MARSHALL, Ineke H. (ed.) (1997) *Minorities, Migrants, and Crime.* London: Sage.

MARTENS, Peter L. (1997) "Immigrants, Crime, and Criminal Justice in Sweden," in M. Tonry (ed.), *Ethnicity, Crime, and Immigration: Comparative and Cross-National Perspectives.* Chicago: University of Chicago Press. pp. 183–255.

MARTIN, Jeffrey T. (2013) "The *Hukou* and Traditional Virtue: An Ethnographic Note on Taiwanese Policing." *Theoretical Criminology* 17: 261–9.

MARTÍNEZ, Daniel E. and Jeremy Slack (2013) "What Part of 'Illegal' Don't You Understand? The Consequences of Criminalizing Unauthorized Mexican Migrants in the United States." *Social and Legal Studies* 22: 535–51.

MARTINEZ, Ramiro Jr and Abel Valenzuela (eds) (2006) *Immigration and Crime: Race, Ethnicity and Violence.* New York: New York University Press.

MARX, Karl (1867 [1967]) *Capital. Volume I.* New York: International Publishers.

MARX, Karl and Friedrich Engels (1848 [1985]) *The Communist Manifesto.* London: Penguin Books.

MASSEY, Douglas S., Jorge Durand and Nolan Malone (2002) *Beyond Smoke and Mirrors. Mexican Immigration in an Era of Economic Integration.* New York: Russell Sage Foundation.

MATHEWS, Gordon (2007) "Chungking Mansions: A Center of Low-End Globalization." *Ethnology* 46: 169–83.

MATZA, David (1964) *Delinquency and Drift.* New York: John Wiley.

MATZA, David (1969) *Becoming Deviant.* Englewood Cliffs, NJ: Prentice-Hall.

MCCULLOCH, Jude and S. Pickering (eds) (2012) *Borders and Crime: Pre-Crime, Mobility and Serious Harm in an Age of Globalization.* Houndmills, Basingstoke: Palgrave Macmillan.

MCDONALD, William (ed.) (2009) *Immigration, Crime and Justice. Sociology of Crime, Law, and Deviance, Volume 13.* Bingley, UK: Emerald/JAI Press.

MEAD, George H. (1934) *Mind, Self, and Society.* Chicago: University of Chicago.

MEAD, George H. (1925 [1964]) "The Genesis of the Self and Social Control," in G. H. Mead, *Selected Writings.* Indianapolis, IL: Bobbs–Merrill. pp. 267–93.

MELOSSI, Dario (1985) "Punishment and Social Action: Changing Vocabularies of Punitive Motive Within a Political Business Cycle." *Current Perspectives in Social Theory* 6: 169–97.

MELOSSI, Dario (1990) *The State of Social Control: A Sociological Study of Concepts of State and Social Control in the Making of Democracy.* Cambridge: Polity Press and New York: St Martin's Press.

MELOSSI, Dario (ed.) (1999) *Multiculturalismo e sicurezza in Emilia-Romagna: prima parte.* Quaderno n. 15 Città Sicure Project, Bologna: Regione Emilia-Romagna.

MELOSSI, Dario (2003a) "'In a Peaceful Life': Migration and the Crime of Modernity in Europe/Italy." *Punishment and Society* 5: 371–97.

MELOSSI, Dario (2003b) "The Simple 'Heuristic Maxim' of an 'Unusual Human Being'. Introduction," in G. Rusche and O. Kirchheimer, *Punishment and Social Structure.* New Brunswick, NJ: Transaction Publishers. pp. 9–46.

MELOSSI, Dario (2005) "Security, Social Control, Democracy and Migration within the 'Constitution' of the EU." *European Law Journal* 11: 5–21.

MELOSSI, Dario (2008) *Controlling Crime, Controlling Society: Thinking About Crime in Europe and America*. Cambridge: Polity Press.

MELOSSI, Dario (2010a) "Thorsten Sellin," in K. Hayward, S. Maruna and J. Mooney (eds), *Fifty Key Thinkers in Criminology*. London: Routledge. pp. 76–82.

MELOSSI, Dario (2010b) "Soliti noti." *Etnografia e ricerca qualitativa* III, 3: 449–58.

MELOSSI, Dario (2010c) "Il diritto della canaglia: teoria del ciclo, migrazioni e diritto." *Studi Sulla Questione Criminale* 5 (2): 51–73.

MELOSSI, Dario (2012) "The Processes of Criminalization of Migrants and the Borders of 'Fortress Europe'," in J. McCulloch and S. Pickering (eds), *Borders and Crime: Pre-Crime, Mobility and Serious Harm in an Age of Globalization*. Houndmills, Basingstoke: Palgrave Macmillan. pp. 17–34.

MELOSSI, Dario (2013a) "Punishment and Migration Between Europe and the USA: A Transnational 'Less Eligibility'?" in J. Simon and R. Sparks (eds), *The SAGE Handbook of Punishment and Society*. London: Sage. pp. 416–33.

MELOSSI, Dario (2013b) "The Borders of the European Union and the Processes of Criminalization of Migrants," in S. Body-Gendrot, M. Hough, K. Kerezsi, R. Lévy and S. Snacken (eds), *The Routledge Handbook of European Criminology*. London and New York: Routledge. pp. 499–513.

MELOSSI, Dario (2013c) "The Processes of Criminalization of Migrants and the Question of Europe as a 'Land of Immigration'," in T. Daems, D. Van Zyl Smit and S. Snacken (eds), *European Penology?* Oxford and Portland, OR: Hart Publishing. pp. 125–44.

MELOSSI, Dario (2013d) "People on the Move: From the Countryside to the Factory/ Prison," in K. Franko Aas and M. Bosworth (eds), *The Borders of Punishment: Migration, Citizenship, and Social Exclusion*. Oxford: Oxford University Press. pp. 273–90.

MELOSSI, Dario and Massimo Pavarini (1977 [1981]) *The Prison and the Factory*. London: Macmillan.

MELOSSI, Dario, Stefania Crocitti, Ester Massa and Dino Gibertoni (2011) *Devianza e immigrazione: una ricerca nelle scuole dell'Emilia-Romagna*. Quaderno n. 37 Città Sicure Project. Bologna: Regione Emilia-Romagna.

MELOSSI, Dario, Alessandro De Giorgi and Ester Massa (2009) "The 'Normality' of 'Second Generations' in Italy and the Importance of Legal Status: A Self-Report Delinquency Study," in W. McDonald (ed.), *Immigration, Crime and Justice. Sociology of Crime, Law, and Deviance* 13. Bingley: Emerald/JAI Press. pp. 47–65.

MENJÍVAR, Cecilia and Leisy J. Abrego (2012) "Legal Violence: Immigration Law and the Lives of Central American Immigrants." *American Journal of Sociology* 117: 1380–421.

MERTON, Robert K. (1938) "Social Structure and Anomie." *American Sociological Review* 3: 672–82.

MEZZADRA, Sandro and Brett Neilson (2013) *Border as Method, or, the Multiplication of Labor*. Durham, NC: Duke University Press.

MOHLER, Henry Calvin (1924–1925) "Convict Labor Policies." *Journal of Criminal Law and Criminology* 15: 530–97.

MONTE, Michela (2002) "Le politiche di immigrazione in Germania: la criminalità degli immigrati di II e III generazione." Laurea Thesis in Criminology, Faculty of Law, University of Bologna, Academic Year 2001–2002.

MORRISON, John (2000) *The Trafficking and Smuggling of Refugees: The End Game in European Asylum Policy*. Geneva: UNHCR.

MORRISON, Wayne (1995) *Theoretical Criminology: From Modernity to Post-Modernism*. London: Cavendish.

NEWBURN, Tim, Paul Lewis and Josephine Metcalf (2011) "A New Kind of Riot? From Brixton 1981 to Tottenham 2011." *The Guardian*, 9 December.

OUSEY, Graham C. and Charis E. Kubrin (2009) "Exploring the Connection between Immigration and Violent Crime Rates in U.S. Cities, 1980–2000." *Social Problems* 56: 447–73.

OXFAM (2005) *Foreign Territory: The Internationalisation of EU Asylum Policy*. Oxford: Oxfam GB.

PAPADEMETRIOU, Demetrios G., Madeleine Sumption and Aaron Terrazas with Carola Burkert, Steven Loyal and Ruth Ferrero-Turrión (2010) *Migration and Immigrants Two Years after the Financial Collapse: Where Do We Stand?* Washington, DC: Migration Policy Institute.

PARK, Robert E. (1922 [1970]) *The Immigrant Press and Its Control*. Westport, CT: Greenwood.

PARK, Robert E. (1928 [1967]) "Human Migration and the Marginal Man," in R. E. Park, *On Social Control and Collective Behaviour*. Chicago: University of Chicago Press. pp. 194–206.

PARK, Robert E. and Ernest W. Burgess (1921 [1969]) *Introduction to the Science of Sociology*. Chicago: University of Chicago Press.

PARK, Robert E., Ernest W. Burgess and Roderick D. McKenzie (1925 [1967]) *The City*. Chicago: University of Chicago Press.

PARMAR, Alpa (2014) "Ethnicities, Racism, and Crime in England and Wales," in S. M. Bucerius and M. Tonry (eds), *Ethnicity, Crime, and Immigration*. New York: Oxford University Press. pp. 321–59

PASSEL, Jeffrey S. (2006) "Size and Characteristics of the Unauthorized Migrant Population in the U.S.: Estimates Based on the March 2005 Current Population Survey." Washington, DC: Pew Research Hispanic Trends Project.

PASSELL, Jeffrey S. and D'Vera Cohn (2010) "U.S. Unauthorized Immigration Flows Are Down Sharply Since Mid-Decade." Washington, DC: Pew Research Center.

PASSEL, Jeffrey S., D'Vera Cohn and Ana Gonzalez-Barrera (2013) "Population Decline of Unauthorized Immigrants Stalls, May Have Reversed, New Estimate: 11.7 million in 2012." Washington, DC: Pew Research Hispanic Trends Project.

PICKERING, Sharon (2014) "Floating Carceral Spaces: Border Enforcement and Gender on the High Seas." *Punishment and Society* 16: 187–205.

PICKERING, Sharon and Leanne Weber (2013) "Policing Transversal Borders," in Katja Franko Aas and Mary Bosworth (eds), *The Borders of Punishment: Migration, Citizenship, and Social Exclusion*. Oxford: Oxford University Press. pp. 93–110.

PICKERING, Sharon, Mary Bosworth and Marie Segrave (2014) "Special Issue: Borders, Gender and Punishment." *Punishment and Society* 16: 131–222.

PIKETTY, Thomas (2013) *Capital in the Twenty-First Century*. Cambridge, MA: Harvard University Press.

PIORE, Michael J. (1979) *Birds of Passage: Migrant Labor and Industrial Societies*. Cambridge: Cambridge University Press.

POLANYI, Karl (1944 [1957]) *The Great Transformation*. Boston, MA: Beacon.

PROUDHON, Pierre-Joseph (1840 [1970]) *What Is Property? An Inquiry into the Principle of Right and Government*. New York: Dover.

RADBRUCH,Gustav (1938) "Der Ursprung des Strafrechts aus dem Stande der Unfreien," in G. Radbruch, *Elegantiae Juris Criminalis*. Basle: Verlag für Recht und Gesellschaft. pp. 1–11.

RAHOLA, Federico (2003) *Zone definitivamente temporanee. I luoghi dell'umanità in eccesso*. Verona: Ombre corte.

RAINERMAN, Craig and Harry G. Levine (1997) *Crack in America: Demon Drugs and Social Justice*. Berkeley: University of California Press.

REX, John and Robert Moore (1967) *Race, Community, and Conflict: A Study of Sparkbrook*. London: Oxford University Press.

RIOS, Victor M. (2011) *Punished: Policing the Lives of Black and Latino Boys*. New York: NYU Press.

ROCK, Paul (2005) "Chronocentrism and British Criminology." *British Journal of Sociology* 56: 473–91.

ROSTAIN, Nathalie (2013) "Criminalità ed immigrazione di seconda e terza generazione in Francia." Laurea Thesis in Criminology. Academic year 2012–2013, School of Law, University of Bologna.

RUGGIERO, Vincenzo (2006) *Understanding Political Violence (Crime and Justice)*. Buckingham: Open University Press.

RUMBAUT, Rubén G. (2008) "Undocumented Immigration and Rates of Crime and Imprisonment: Popular Myths and Empirical Realities." Paper presented to the Police Foundation National Conference on "The Role of Local Police: Striking a Balance Between Immigration Enforcement and Civil Liberties", Washington, DC, August 21–22.

RUMBAUT, Rubén G. and Walter A. Ewing (2007) *The Myth of Immigrant Criminality and the Paradox of Assimilation: Incarceration Rates among Native and Foreign-Born Men*. Washington, DC: Immigration Policy Center.

RUMBAUT, Rubén G. and Alejandro Portes (eds) (2001) *Ethnicities: Children of Immigrants in America*. Berkeley: University of California Press.

RUMBAUT, Rubén G., Roberto G. Gonzales, Golnaz Komaie, Charlie V. Morgan and Rosaura Tafoya-Estrada (2006) "Immigration and Incarceration: Patterns and Predictors of Imprisonment among First- and Second-Generation Young Adults," in R. Martinez Jr and A. Valenzuela (eds), *Immigration and Crime: Race, Ethnicity and Violence*. New York: New York University Press. pp. 64–89.

RUSCHE, Georg and Otto Kirchheimer (1939 [2003]) *Punishment and Social Structure*. New Brunswick, NJ: Transaction Books.

SABOL, William J. (1989) "Racially Disproportionate Prison Population in the United States." *Contemporary Crises* 13: 405–32.

SAEZ, Emmanuel (2009) "Striking It Richer: The Evolution of Top Incomes in the United States" (Update with 2007 estimates). Working Paper Series, Institute for Research on Labor and Employment, University of California Berkeley.

SAEZ, Emmanuel and Thomas Piketty (2003) "Income Inequality in the United States, 1913–1998." *Quarterly Journal of Economics* 118: 1–39.

SALVATORE, Ricardo D. and Carlos Aguirre (eds) (1996) *The Birth of the Penitentiary in Latin America: Essays on Criminology, Prison Reform, and Social Control, 1830–1940*. Austin: University of Texas Press.

SAMPSON, Robert J. (2006) "Open Doors Don't Invite Criminals." *The New York Times*, March 11.

SAMPSON, Robert J. (2008) "Rethinking Crime and Immigration." *Contexts* 7 (1): 28–33.

SAMPSON, Robert J. (2012) *Great American City: Chicago and the Enduring Neighborhood Effect*. Chicago: University of Chicago Press.

SASSEN, Saskia (1991) *The Global City: New York, London, Tokyo.* Princeton: Princeton University Press.

SASSEN, Saskia (2010) "Immigration: Control vs Governance." Available at: www.opendemocracy.net.

SAYAD, Abdelmalek (1999 [2004]) *The Suffering of the Immigrant.* Cambridge: Polity Press.

SCHUTZ, Alfred (1944) "The Stranger: An Essay in Social Psychology." *American Journal of Sociology* 49: 499–507.

SCULL, Andrew T. (1977) *Decarceration: Community Treatment and the Deviant – A Radical View.* Englewood Cliffs, NJ: Prentice-Hall.

SEGRAVE, Marie, Sanja Milivojevic and Sharon Pickering (2009) *Sex Trafficking: International Context and Response.* Uffculme: Willan.

SELLIN, Thorsten (1937) *Research Memorandum on Crime in the Depression.* New York: Social Science Research Council.

SELLIN, Thorsten (1938) *Culture Conflict and Crime.* New York: Social Science Research Council.

SELLIN, Thorsten (1944) *Pioneering in Penology.* Philadelphia: University of Pennsylvania Press.

SELLIN, Thorsten (1976) *Slavery and the Penal System.* New York: Elsevier.

SERENI, Emilio (1948) *Il capitalismo nelle campagne (1860–1900).* Turin: Einaudi.

SHARP, Clare and Tracey Budd (2005) *Minority Groups and Crime: Findings from the Offending Crime and Justice Survey 2003.* Home Office Online Report 33/05. London: Home Office.

SHAW, Clifford and Henry D. McKay (1942) *Juvenile Delinquency and Urban Areas.* Chicago: University of Chicago Press.

SHERMAN, Larry W. (1993) "Defiance, Deterrence, and Irrelevance: A Theory of the Criminal Sanction." *Journal of Research in Crime and Delinquency* 30: 445–73.

SHIBUTANI, Tamotsu (1962) "Reference Groups and Social Control," in A. M. Rose (ed.), *Human Behavior and Social Processes.* Boston: Houghton Mifflin. pp. 128–47.

SIMES, Jessica T. and Mary C. Waters (2014) "The Politics of Immigration and Crime," in S. M. Bucerius and M. Tonry (eds), *Ethnicity, Crime, and Immigration.* New York: Oxford University Press. pp. 457–83.

SIMMEL, Georg (1908 [1971]) "The Stranger," in G. Simmel, *On Individuality and Social Forms.* Chicago: University of Chicago Press. pp. 143–9.

SIMON, Jonathan (2014a) *Mass Incarceration on Trial: A Remarkable Court Decision and the Future of Prisons in America.* New York: New Press.

SIMON, Jonathan (2014b) "A Radical Need for Criminology." *Social Justice* 40 (1–2): 9–23.

SISKIN, Alison (2012) *Immigration-Related Detention: Current Legislative Issues.* Congress Research Service Report for Congress, January 12. Washington, DC: CRS.

SLOAN, Cle (2006) *Bastards of the Party* (film, USA).

SMITH, David (1997) "Ethnic Origins, Crime, and Criminal Justice in England and Wales," in M. Tonry (ed.), *Ethnicity, Crime, and Immigration: Comparative and Cross-National Perspectives.* Chicago: University of Chicago Press. pp. 101–82.

SNACKEN, Sonja (2010) "Resisting Punitiveness in Europe?" *Theoretical Criminology* 14: 273–92.

SOLIVETTI, Luigi M. (2010) *Immigration, Social Integration and Crime: A Cross-National Approach.* Abingdon and New York: Routledge.

SOLIVETTI, Luigi M. (2012) "Looking for a Fair Country: Features and Determinants of Immigrants' Involvement in Crime in Europe." *Howard Journal of Criminal Justice* 51: 133–59.

SOLIVETTI, Luigi M. (2013) *Immigrazione società e crimine: dati e considerazioni sul caso Italia*. Bologna: il Mulino.

STONEQUIST, Everett V. (1937 [1961]) *The Marginal Man*. New York: Russell and Russell.

STOWELL, Jacob I. (2007) *Immigration and Crime: Considering the Direct and Indirect Effects of Immigration on Violent Criminal Behavior*. New York: LFB Scholarly Press.

STOWELL, Jacob I., Steven F. Messner, Kelly F. McGeever and Lawrence E. Raffalovich (2009) "Immigration and the Recent Violent Crime Drop in the United States: A Pooled, Cross-Sectional Time-Series Analysis of Metropolitan Areas." *Criminology* 47: 889–928.

STUMPF, Juliet P. (2006) "The Crimmigration Crisis: Immigrants, Crime, and Sovereign Power." *American University Law Review* 56: 367–419.

STUMPF, Juliet P. (2013) "The Process Is the Punishment in Crimmigration Law," in Katja Franko Aas and Mary Bosworth (eds), *The Borders of Punishment: Migration, Citizenship, and Social Exclusion*. Oxford: Oxford University Press. pp. 58–75.

SULLIVAN, Mercer L. (1989) *Getting Paid: Youth Crime and Work in the Inner City*. New York: Cornell University Press.

SUTHERLAND, Edwin H. (1924) *Criminology*. Philadelphia: Lippincott.

SUTHERLAND, Edwin (1934 [1956]) "The Decreasing Prison Population of England," in Albert Cohen, Alfred Lindesmith and Karl Schüssler (eds), *The Sutherland Papers*. Bloomington: Indiana University Press. pp. 200–26.

SUTHERLAND, Edwin H. (1937) *The Professional Thief*. Chicago: University of Chicago Press.

SUTHERLAND, Edwin H. (1942 [1973]) "Development of the Theory," in Edwin H. Sutherland, *On Analyzing Crime*. Chicago: University of Chicago Press. pp. 13–29.

SUTHERLAND, Edwin H. and Donald R. Cressey (1978) *Criminology*. Philadelphia: Lippincott.

TAKAKI, Ronald (1979) *Iron Cages: Race and Culture in 19th-Century America*. New York: Knopf.

TETI, Vito (1993) *La razza maledetta: origini del pregiudizio antimeridionale*. Rome: Manifestolibri.

THOMAS, William and Florian Znaniecki (1918–20) *The Polish Peasant in Europe and America*. Chicago: University of Chicago Press.

THOMPSON, Edward P. (1971) "The Moral Economy of the English Crowd in the Eighteenth Century." *Past and Present* 50: 76–136.

THRASHER, Frederic M. (1927) *The Gang*. Chicago: University of Chicago Press.

TONRY, Michael (ed.) (1997) *Ethnicity, Crime, and Immigration: Comparative and Cross-National Perspectives*. Chicago: University of Chicago Press.

TOURNIER, Pierre (1997) "Nationality, Crime, and Criminal Justice in France," in M. Tonry (ed.), *Ethnicity, Crime, and Immigration: Comparative and Cross-National Perspectives*. Chicago: University of Chicago Press. pp. 523–51.

UGELVIK, Thomas (2013) "Seeing Like a Welfare State: Immigration Control, Statecraft, and a Prison with Double Vision," in Katja Franko Aas and Mary Bosworth (eds), *The Borders of Punishment: Migration, Citizenship, and Social Exclusion*. Oxford: Oxford University Press. pp. 183–98.

UGELVIK, Thomas (2014) "Paternal Pains of Imprisonment: Incarcerated Fathers, Ethnic Minority Masculinity and Resistance Narratives." *Punishment & Society* 16: 152–68.

VAN DER LEUN, Joanne (2003) *Looking for Loopholes: Processes of Incorporation of Illegal Immigrants in the Netherlands*. Amsterdam: Amsterdam University Press.

VAN DIJK, Teun A. (1993) *Elite Discourse and Racism.* London: Sage.

VAN ZYL SMIT, Dirk and Sonja Snacken (2009) *Principles of European Prison Law and Policy: Penology and Human Rights.* Oxford: Oxford University Press.

VARGAS, José (2011) "Two decades of living a lie in America." *International Herald Tribune* June 25–26.

VECCHIO, Francesco (2014) *Asylum Seeking and the Global City.* London: Routledge.

VENKATESH, Sudhir (2008) *Gang Leader for a Day: A Rogue Sociologist Takes to the Streets.* New York: Penguin.

VIGNESWARAN, Darshan (2013) "Making Mobility a Problem: How South African Officials Criminalize Migration," in Katja Franko Aas and Mary Bosworth (eds), *The Borders of Punishment: Migration, Citizenship, and Social Exclusion.* Oxford: Oxford University Press. pp. 111–27.

WACQUANT, Loïc (2006) *Urban Outcasts: A Comparative Sociology of Advanced Marginality.* Cambridge: Polity Press.

WACQUANT, Loïc (2009) *Punishing the Poor. The Neoliberal Government of Social Insecurity.* Durham, NC: Duke University Press.

WALKLATE, Sandra and Karen Evans (1999) *Zero Tolerance or Community Tolerance? Managing Crime in High Crime Areas.* Aldershot: Ashgate.

WALLERSTEIN, Immanuel (1974) *The Modern World-System, Vol. I: Capitalist Agriculture and the Origins of the European World-Economy in the Sixteenth Century.* New York/London: Academic Press.

WALZER, Michael (1983) *Spheres of Justice: A Defense of Pluralism and Equality.* New York: Basic Books.

WANG, Fei-Ling (2004) "Reformed Migration Control and New Targeted People: China's *Hukou* System in the 2000s." *The China Quarterly* 177: 115–32.

WARREN, Robert (2014) "Democratizing Data about Unauthorized Residents in the United States: Estimates and Public-Use Data, 2010 to 2013." *Journal on Migration and Human Security* 2: 305–28.

WEBER, Leanne (2012) "Policing a World in Motion," in Jude McCulloch and S. Pickering (eds), *Borders and Crime: Pre-Crime, Mobility and Serious Harm in an Age of Globalization.* Houndmills, Basingstoke: Palgrave Macmillan. pp. 35–53.

WEBER, Leanne and Ben Bowling (2008) "Valiant Beggars and Global Vagabonds: Select, Eject, Immobilize." *Theoretical Criminology* 12: 355–75.

WESTERN, Bruce (2006) *Punishment and Inequality in America.* New York: Russell Sage Foundation.

WHYTE, William Foote (1943) *Street Corner Society: The Social Structure of an Italian Slum.* Chicago: University of Chicago Press.

WICKERSHAM COMMISSION (1931) National Commission on Law Observance and Enforcement. *Crime and the Foreign Born.* Washington: US Government Printing Office. Report No. 10. (Republished in 1968 by Patterson Smith, Montclair, New Jersey.)

WILKERSON, Isabel (2010) *The Warmth of Other Suns: The Epic Story of America's Great Migration.* New York: Random House.

WILSON, William Julius Wilson (1987) *The Truly Disadvantaged: The Inner City, the Underclass and Public Policy.* Chicago: University of Chicago Press.

WRIGHT, Richard (1940 [1987]) *Native Son.* New York: Harper & Row.

WRIGHT, Richard (1944 [2008]) *Black Boy.* New York: Harper Perennial Modern Classics.

WU, Xiaogang and Donald J.Treiman (2004) "The Household Registration System and Social Stratification in China: 1955–1996." *Demography* 41: 363–84.

XU, Jianhua (2009) "The Robbery of Motorcycle Taxi Drivers in China: A Lifestyle/Routine Activity Perspective and Beyond." *British Journal of Criminology* 49: 491–512.

YAMAMOTO, Ryoko and David T. Johnson (2014) "The Convergence of Control: Immigration and Crime in Contemporary Japan," in S. M. Bucerius and M. Tonry (eds), *Ethnicity, Crime, and Immigration.* New York: Oxford University Press. pp. 738–65.

YOUNG, Jock (1999) *The Exclusive Society.* London: Sage.

YOUNG, Jock (2003) "To These Wet and Windy Shores: Recent Immigration Policy in the UK." *Punishment and Society* 5: 449–62.

YOUNG, Jock (2007) *The Vertigo of Late Modernity.* London: Sage.

ZEDNER, Lucia (2013) "Is the Criminal Law Only for Citizens? A Problem at the Borders of Punishment," in Katja Franko Aas and Mary Bosworth (eds), *The Borders of Punishment: Migration, Citizenship, and Social Exclusion.* Oxford: Oxford University Press. pp. 40–57.

ZHONG, Lena Y. (2009) *Communities, Crime and Social Capital in Contemporary China.* Uffculme: Willan.

index

cosmopolitanism, 49
Cressey, Donald R., 30
crime, definitions of, 2
Criminal Man (Lombroso), 1
criminal propensities, 39
Criminal Sociology (Ferri), 10
Criminology (Sutherland), 40
Critcher, Chas, 55
Crocitti, Stefania, 52
culture conflicts, 19, 20–21, 29–30, 62
Culture of Control (Garland), 80

Davis, Angela, 24, 77, 85–86
De Blasio, Bill, 44n19
Department of Homeland Security (US),
    42n15
deportation, 35–36, 42
Dewey, John, 13
Diamanti, Ilvo, 74
differential association theory, 29–33
Dillinger, John, 23
Doty, Roxanne L., 44
downward assimilation, 38, 39–41
Dreiser, Theodor, 18
Du Bois, W.E.B., 31
Dublin rule, 73
Durkheim, Emile, 2, 14

economic crisis, 63–66
enclosures of common land, 6
enemy penology (*Feindstrafrecht*), 72
Engels, Friedrich, 8, 10
England, 3, 6, 7, 48, 54–56, 87
Erikson, Kai, 71
ethnic enclaves, 18, 32
ethnic niches, 38
Ethnicity, Crime, and Immigration (Tonry),
    48–49
Europe
    criminalization of migrants in, 49–57, 80
    economic crisis in, 63–66
    emigration in, 47–49
    Fordism and Taylorism in, 26–27
    history of migration in, x–xi, 6–12
    immigration policies in, 70–75
    imprisonment of migrants in, 33–34,
        66–70, **67–68**, 87–88
    police and migrants in, 57–60

Europe *cont.*
    self-report surveys in, 60–63
    undocumented migrants in, 35, 63–64,
        87–88
    See also specific countries
European Commission, 65–66
European Court of Human Rights, 71
European Union (EU), 4, 89–90
Ewing, Walter A., 38

Fabini, Giulia, 53, 57–58
Federn, Paul, 20n6
Ferraris, Valeria, 52, 53
Ferri, Enrico, 10–11
Fitzgerald, Marian, 55
Ford, Henry, 26
Fordism, 26–27, 33, 48–49
Fortress Europe, 66n20, 74–75
Foucault, Michel, 7, 8, 24n9
France, 48, 54, 58, 69, 87
Frontex, 72–74

gang organizations, 21–23
The Gangs of New York (Asbury), 12
Garland, David, 80
Gartner, Rosemary, 44, 59
Germany, 3, 48–49, 52n4, 78, 87, 89
Giddens, Anthony, 9
Gilroy, Paul, 55, 63n14
globalization, 31, 32–33, 49, 77–80
Gobineau, Arthur de, 19–20
Goffman, Alice, 41n12
Goldman, Emma, 14
Graeber, David, 33
Graham, John, 61
Gulf Cooperation Council, 78

Hagan, John, 31
Hall, Stuart, 55
Hammar, Tomas, 72
Harcourt, Bernard, 58
Hirschi, Travis, 60–61
The Hobo (Anderson), 14, 18
Hobsbawm, Eric, 86
Homeland Security Act (US, 2002), 42
Hong Kong, 81–82
Hoover, John Edgar, 14, 23
human trafficking, 81–82